Preparing to Become a Bride

By Studying the Fruit of the Spirit

Felicia Ann

FRUITFUL
VINE
PRESS

Preparing to Become a Bride by Studying the Fruit of the Spirit

© 2025 by Felicia Ann

All rights reserved. No part of this book may be reproduced, distributed, or transmitted in any form or by any means, including photocopying, recording, or other electronic or mechanical methods, without the prior written permission of the publisher, except in the case of brief quotations embodied in critical reviews and certain other noncommercial uses permitted by copyright law.

Scripture quotations are taken from the [insert Bible translation(s) used—e.g., King James Version (KJV) or New International Version (NIV)]. Used by permission. All rights reserved.

ISBN: 979-8-218-78887-2

Published by Fruitful Vine Press

Atlanta, GA

Cover design by Todd Schowalter

Printed in the United States of America

First Edition

Library of Congress Cataloging-in-Publication Data (CIP)

Ann, Felicia

Preparing to Become a Bride by Studying the Fruit of the Spirit / Felicia Ann. — 1st ed.

p. cm.

ISBN 979-8-218-78887-2

Marriage - Religious aspects - Christianity.

Wives - Religious life.

Fruit of the Spirit - Biblical teaching.

Christian women - Religious life.

I. Preparing to Become a Bride by Studying the Fruit of the Spirit

Table of Contents

Introduction 11

My Personal Journey 13

Fundamental – God Gave Us the Blueprint of a Wife 16

Fundamental – God's House Rules 21

Fundamental – What is your Vision? 24

Fundamental – God Established Marriage Roles 27

Fundamental – The Role of the Husband 31

Fundamental – God is the Head of the Home 34

Fundamental – The Bible Defines Marriage as a Covenant 38

Fundamental – God Hates Divorce 40

Fruit of the Spirit – God Is Our Spiritual Fruit Basket 44

Fruit of the Spirit – Love 45

Fruit of the Spirit – Joy 52

Fruit of the Spirit – Peace 56

Fruit of the Spirit – Kindness 59

Fruit of the Spirit – Goodness 62

Fruit of the Spirit – Forbearance 65

Fruit of the Spirit – Gentleness 69

Fruit of the Spirit – Faithfulness 71

Fruit of the Spirit – Self-Control 74

Fruit of the Spirit - Patience 78

Preparing for Marriage 82
Preparing for Marriage – Trusting God While Remaining Patient . 84
Preparing for Marriage – Premarital Counseling 86
Preparing for Marriage – Be You 88
Preparing for Marriage - Communication 91
Preparing for Marriage – Friendships 94
Preparing for Marriage – Being a Helpmeet 98
Preparing for Marriage – Choices 101
Preparing for Marriage – Order 103
Workbook - Self-Reflection Questions 106
Workbook - Discussion Questions for a Couple 111
Epilogue 118
About the Author 120

Dedications

One of our deepest desires is for someone to think we are truly special.

- **Felicia Ann**

I dedicate this book to Yah, my Lord and Savior, Jesus Christ.

Because He died for my sins, I am forgiven and reborn.

THANK YOU SO MUCH, GOD! You are truly an amazing, loving Father! I am absolutely NOTHING without YOU!

I now have the mindset to understand God's will for my life in a way that was not known to me before I was redeemed by His blood. He is the author and the finisher. With His guidance, I have been able to express His love and desires through this book. Although this book was birthed through pain, I was able to find MY purpose and obtain HIS definition of joy!

Thank you, God… you are so good and so faithful! I am honored that you call me friend, and I love you so very much! THANK YOU for always giving me your best and showing me agape love!

To my parents, Adell and Bessie High Young, who are no longer on Earth. Watching my parents both go after their dreams so passionately inspired me to know that I can do anything if I work hard and stay the course. My dad was a black entrepreneur in a small town in the early 1960s. My mom was an educator who achieved her master's in education all while caring for her husband and two small children. Life was not a crystal stair; yet they both climbed it with blood, sweat and tears. They didn't give up, despite adversity. Because of them, neither will I! Watching them work together helped me to define "bone of my bone, flesh of my flesh". I love you so very much Mama and Daddy! You will live inside of my beating heart FOREVER! THANK YOU for being the absolute best parents to me!

To my daughter, Kira, who taught me love on another level. It was through your birth that I experienced a mother's love. I now understand the unconditional love that God has for us as His children. Your words of encouragement led me to read the Bible on a daily basis. As a result, my life began to transform. God used you to help mold me into the person that He created me to be. Kira, your very existence birthed my God-given purpose! I made a lot of mistakes while raising you because I was not living in the will of God. I want to thank you for forgiving me. Your walk in Christ and your forgiveness has inspired me to become a better version of myself and I am so grateful that God chose you to teach me. I love you with all of my beating heart and I will continue to work on myself so that together we can break generational curses and be rewarded with our Godly inheritances. I love you so very much! THANK YOU for your patience and understanding while Yah worked on me!

To my three beautiful Yah blessings: Jayden, Railey and Bella. Each of you has a special place in my heart. You accepted me and called me Mommy! You are each so full of love. The innocence of your love made me want to be a better version of myself. I saw a second chance to be redeemed through your love. I desired to give you a healed part of me in hopes that each of you would be healed. I am grateful to have been a part of your lives and to have had the opportunity to watch you grow. You are each uniquely and wonderfully made with individual gifts that the world needs. Thank you so much for being patient with me while I worked on healing. I am grateful that you each continue to love me and forgive me for my shortcomings. I am so thankful for your hugs and the inner parts of your souls that have made a connection with mine. I love you all so very much!

To Mama K: I just love you! You became a mom and a friend to me during a time when I was lost, lonely and depressed. You were always there when I called, and you reminded me of the faithfulness of God. You encouraged me to keep trusting God and to not settle. You have no idea how much I appreciate your wisdom and love for God; it has blessed my soul. You are truly a gift from God and I am so grateful for you and your love. THANK YOU for stepping in to be such an amazing mother figure and calling me your **Sunshine**! I love you so very much!

To my Best Buddy 4 Life, Kathy, you have been NOTHING but AMAZING during some of the darkest times in my life. You have encouraged me, prayed for me and loved me. You showed up for me and gave me life lessons through God's love that magnified what I love most about your friendship. From the bottom of my heart, I love and appreciate YOU! I am so grateful to walk this thing called life out with you. You are more than a friend…you are my **BB4L (Best Buddy 4 Life)** and my sister! THANK YOU for the long encouraging talks and your undivided love for me!! I love you so very much, My BB4L!

To my friend and Bible study partner, Valerie. Thank you, Val, for your dedication to our Bible study. It was your dedication to stay the course that helped me to connect the dots in so many areas. In addition, your love and friendship were an instrumental piece of the puzzle. Thank you for your spiritual insight and perseverance, it has been such a motivation. I love you so very much, Val!

To my friend, Erica-thank you so much for your encouragement. Your friendship was nothing short of RIGHT ON TIME. You came into my life, poured into me and checked on me and showed me love. You stayed on me to complete this book, and I truly appreciate YOU! Prayerfully, you will find nuggets in this book to prepare you to walk down the aisle one day 😊 I love you so very much, friend. Thank you for being YOU!

To my friend Kisha, God whispered your name and instructed us to "Heal Together". Now look at what the Lord has done! He is healing our trauma and our broken hearts. This is truly a full circle moment! What an AWESOME God we serve! I am grateful for your long-standing friendship throughout the years and your beautiful heart. I am beyond grateful to witness your testimony unfold. I am so proud of you! I love you so very much, friend!

To Timothy Dance, last but not least, none of this would have been possible without you and Yah! I wasn't prepared to be a wife, but you saw me as one. I truly want to thank you for choosing to never give up on us. Thank you for helping me discover me and trying your best to support my dreams. I am truly grateful for our journey...I will always love you, Tim!

A special thank you to my illustrator, Todd, and my editor, Stacy. Without the two of you, this vision would have perished. I know without a shadow of a doubt that God placed you both in my life for such a time as this! I would be remiss not to give you both the flowers that you each deserve. Thank you from the bottom of my heart for helping me water the seeds that God placed upon my heart. You are both instrumental in making my vision a reality! I'm eternally grateful for both of you! My heart is so full!

Introduction

Focus on the "become" and not the "outcome."

- **Pastor Myron Golden**

The book *Preparing to Become a Bride by Studying the Fruit of the Spirit* was birthed through my desire to understand marriage. Love, relationships and especially marriage are quite complicated and I was failing at it. Honestly, I was exhausted from the continuous hurt and the scarring that failing left on my heart.

This prompted me to reach out for help. I reached out to the Creator, my Father in Heaven, for His guidance and understanding. After all, He created marriage, so who better to seek direction from?!

He directed me to go back to *The Beginning*. He directed me back to the Garden of Eden when man and woman were first created. He gave me spiritual revelation on how He created us to function in His Kingdom and reminded me that His laws/commandants were literally set in stone–for a reason. He guided me to the gifts He gave me through the Holy Spirit.

The truth is that none of us are fully aware of how to become a wife. Personally, I was oblivious. I was limited by my own upbringing. I had only the marriages of friends, the false narratives on TV/reality shows, and the trial and error of my own personal failure.

Spending time with God, and understanding who He is and who He created us to be, put things into perspective. The unknown became clearer simply by spending time in His word. Now, I am choosing to become a wife by studying the Fruit of the Spirit.

As I studied and prayed, I began to see how the word of God in the beginning, combined with Jesus' teachings, could provide the help I needed. As I dove deeper into His scripture, using it to help me in my own marriage, I began to see how this could potentially help others.

This book is designed for women of faith who desire marriage, starting their marriage or are looking to strengthen their relationship with their spouse. In addition to providing the Biblical framework for marriage and how to use the gifts of the Holy Spirit in marriage, this book provides scriptures, prayers and personal insights. Through the word of God and self-reflection, my hope is that readers will grow closer to their husbands—and to God.

The book is divided into four sections: Fundamentals, Fruit of the Spirit, Preparing for Marriage, and a Workbook. Each section contains related scripture, as this book is based in God's teaching. The Fundamentals section covers the key components of marriage that God established for us. The Fruit of the Spirit section provides more context for these wonderful gifts God gave to His people. The Preparing for Marriage section provides practical exercises and reflections that can help you as you prepare to be a Godly wife. Finally, the Workbook section should be used as a starting point to help you understand yourself and your partner as you contemplate marriage or seek to strengthen your marriage.

Being a wife is not who you are, it's who you become.

- **Felicia Ann**

My Personal Journey

My journey started with my personal pitfalls. My sins were taking over and getting the best of me. I was not only failing in my relationships, but I was causing additional emotional turmoil within my life.

I began to self-soothe by partying as a means of distraction. But no party helped fill the void and eradicate the pain that was deep inside. I was continually looking for guidance from others but was neglecting to go to our Father in Heaven. I was spending time seeking the things of the world instead of seeking first the Kingdom of Heaven.

I will admit, I was having "fun" while engaging in worldly activities; or at least I thought I was. My definition of "fun" ended in what the world refers to as "karma". I now understand that karma is what the Bible calls "reaping". Therefore, I was reaping what I sowed. I was sowing sin, so I was reaping the consequences of my sin. My disobedience caused self-doubt, trauma and, often, depression.

I began to reflect on my life. I was raised in church. I loved God. I was trying to be a "good" person. I could not understand why I could not find love, joy, peace, or happiness!

I stopped seeking answers from the world and went in consecration with God. I asked Him to give me the blueprint for His love. I asked Him to help me understand what I was doing wrong. I asked Him to explain to me how, if love is something that

He created and something that we all desire to experience, why it is so hard to find a lasting, enduring love.

I began to hear God speak. He told me to go back to the beginning! He wanted me to focus on the breakdown that took place in the Garden of Eden.

As I studied, I realized that Adam and Eve are you and I. Like us, they were created in God's image to do God's work. The one ask that God gave them—and that still applies to you and I—was to remain obedient!

What I recognized is that everywhere we go, there are rules that we must follow. There are/were rules within our parents' and grandparents' homes. We have rules within our community. We have rules within our homes. And, most importantly, there are rules within God's Kingdom. We cannot do whatever we please if it is not pleasing to our Heavenly Father. We cannot make excuses for our disobedience and keep expecting God to forgive our outright disrespect.

As I studied and spent time with God, I realized that I had forsaken the rules that God laid out for His people. For me, I was flat-out disobedient and disrespectful. I needed to clean up my act!

Although I am and will always be a work in progress, I am dedicated to remaining obedient to Our Heavenly Father. It's our obedience that pleases God and governs His blessings. I learned from first-hand experience that temporary pleasure, when in disobedience to God's rules, only creates harm to our mind, body and soul.

Jesus died for our sins, and He is the ultimate sacrifice. I realized that if I continued to live solely through my fleshly desires, I would be taking His sacrifice for granted. God's grace and mercy is a gift, one that I should treasure with gratitude. Jesus did His part and now it was time for me to do mine.

So, here I am! A continuous work in progress. However, instead of looking for "fun" in the world, I look for peace with Jesus.

I have learned how to find peace within my domain, both within my heart, as well as inside of my home. I sit with our Father and spend time with Him daily. I ask Him to work on my heart posture and change me so that I can be used by Him.

Although I feel unworthy, He continues to tell me that I am worth it. Through His patience, forgiveness, love, gentleness, goodness, and kindness, I now have joy, peace and self-control. Because He is Love, I began to love myself. I also have an understanding of what true love looks like as He continues to show me through others who have a heart for Him. Jesus' sacrifice reaped an abundance of good fruit. As a result, I now understand how to harvest the Fruit of the Spirit! Thank you, God.

What is fruit? According to Encyclopaedia Britannica, a fruit is the ripened ovary of a flower that contains seeds and helps disperse them. The ovary is the reproductive structure of the flower that protects the ovules until they are fertilized and turn into seeds (Encyclopaedia Britannica, n.d.).

We are carriers of the seed. As you seek God's guidance, you are led to a land that flows with milk and honey. Allowing seed to land on fertile ground will produce healthy, nutritious, ripened fruit.

- **Felicia Ann**

Fundamental – God Gave Us the Blueprint of a Wife

As our Creator, God had a clear plan for marriage. Rather than having us flounder as we struggled to understand His plan, He gave us a role model in Proverbs 31. He gave us the blueprint to follow as we seek to be Godly women and supportive wives.

Proverbs 31 (NIV)

The Wife of Noble Character

¹⁰ A wife of noble character who can find?
She is worth far more than rubies.
¹¹ Her husband has full confidence in her
and lacks nothing of value.
¹² She brings him good, not harm,
all the days of her life.
¹³ She selects wool and flax
and works with eager hands.
¹⁴ She is like the merchant ships,
bringing her food from afar.
¹⁵ She gets up while it is still night;
she provides food for her family
and portions for her female servants.
¹⁶ She considers a field and buys it;
out of her earnings she plants a vineyard.
¹⁷ She sets about her work vigorously;
her arms are strong for her tasks.
¹⁸ She sees that her trading is profitable,

and her lamp does not go out at night.
¹⁹ In her hand she holds the distaff
and grasps the spindle with her fingers.
²⁰ She opens her arms to the poor
and extends her hands to the needy.
²¹ When it snows, she has no fear for her household;
for all of them are clothed in scarlet.
²² She makes coverings for her bed;
she is clothed in fine linen and purple.
²³ Her husband is respected at the city gate,
where he takes his seat among the elders of the land.
²⁴ She makes linen garments and sells them,
and supplies the merchants with sashes.
²⁵ She is clothed with strength and dignity;
she can laugh at the days to come.
²⁶ She speaks with wisdom,
and faithful instruction is on her tongue.
²⁷ She watches over the affairs of her household
and does not eat the bread of idleness.
²⁸ Her children arise and call her blessed;
her husband also, and he praises her:
²⁹ "Many women do noble things,
but you surpass them all."
³⁰ Charm is deceptive, and beauty is fleeting;
but a woman who fears the Lord is to be praised.
³¹ Honor her for all that her hands have done,
and let her works bring her praise at the city gate.

The poem of a virtuous woman is an ideal blueprint of a Godly wife. It details the characteristics of the wife that we should strive to be.

A virtuous woman possesses all of the Godly characters that make her fruitful. She is loved by her husband, praised by her children and respected by her community.

She is a pillar in her community, giving to those who are less fortunate.

The Proverbs 31 woman is organically fruitful because her desire is to first love God and to seek God in her endeavors. The love that flows throughout her life is a result of the vine that she is connected to, which is Our Heavenly Father. Therefore, she grows good fruit in every area of her life.

Verse 21 speaks of her trust in the Lord by mentioning her response to a snowstorm. It describes her lack of worry about the storm arising because she has placed her trust in the Lord. Also, she is not concerned about a storm affecting her household because she knows that her home is clothed in scarlet. She is not stressed with life's adversity because, through her personal relationship with God, she knows that her household is covered in the blood of Jesus. She has confidence in God and His provisions for her and her family.

Being a Godly woman requires you to have the right priorities, and it starts with nurturing your relationship with God. Seek God, obey God, trust in God and rest in God. He will make every area of your life fruitful.

A Proverbs 31 woman is confident in her role as a wife and is also praised by her husband for her commitments. **Proverbs 31:11 (NIV) says, her husband has full confidence in her and lacks nothing of value.**

The Proverbs 31 woman represents her husband everywhere she goes. She respects God and her husband.

As a result, she dresses modestly. She is sure to dress in attire that is not revealing. She does not seek attention, especially the kind that could lead to unwarranted disrespect, from those that she encounters.

1 Timothy 2:9-10 (NIV) says, I also want women to dress modestly, with decency and propriety, adorning themselves, not with elaborate hairstyles or gold or pearls or expensive clothes, but with good deeds, appropriate for women who profess to worship God.

We have access to numerous options in clothing, accessories and eye-catching hairstyles. In the age of social media, there may be perceived pressure to wear trendy and fashionable styles. However, according to the instructions from the Bible, we are to dress appropriately. Our self-worth and love for God should be the shiny thing that attracts others to us and not our outwardly material possessions.

Verse 10 of Proverbs 31 also describes the ideal woman as being worth far more than rubies. A ruby is one of the most popular traditional jewelry gems and is very durable. Through the ages, the ruby has represented nobility, purity, and passion. From ancient times to modern-day, rubies have been valued by cultures around the world. As one of the world's most precious stones, it still does not compare to the gem of the Proverbs 31 woman. There is no one like her and her value is priceless! She cannot be imitated or duplicated; she is original and irreplaceable. She is truly a valuable asset to her family, her community and to herself. She has done the work to set herself apart from others and what she possesses makes her uniquely and wonderfully made. She is a wise woman!

As you work to prepare to become a wife, take this as a reminder to choose to be a rare jewel.

Fundamental – God's House Rules

We are to follow the laws that He has created and set in place within His Kingdom to assist us in living a harmonious life. Just as His Spirit is alive and well in us today, so are the laws that God commanded us to follow in the Old Testament and from *The Beginning*. Those laws are known as the Ten Commandments:

The 10 Commandments – Exodus 20:2-17 (NIV):

1. "I am the Lord your God, who brought you out of Egypt, out of the land of slavery. You shall have no other gods before me.

2. "You shall not make for yourself an image in the form of anything in heaven above or on the Earth beneath or in the waters below. You shall not bow down to them or worship them; for I, the Lord your God, am a jealous God, punishing the children for the sin of the parents to the third and fourth generation of those who hate me, but showing love to a thousand generations of those who love me and keep my commandments.

3. "You shall not misuse the name of the Lord our God, for the Lord will not hold anyone guiltless who misuses his name.

4. "Remember the Sabbath day by keeping it holy. Six days you shall labor and do all your work, but the seventh day is a sabbath to the Lord your God. On it you shall not do any work, neither you, nor your son or daughter, nor your male or female servant, nor your animals, nor any foreigner residing in your towns. For in six days the Lord made the

heavens and the Earth, the sea, and all that is in them, but he rested on the seventh day. Therefore the Lord blessed the Sabbath day and made it holy.

5. "Honor your father and your mother, so that you may live long in the land the Lord your God is giving you.
6. "You shall not murder.
7. "You shall not commit adultery.
8. "You shall not steal.
9. "You shall not give false testimony against your neighbor.
10. "You shall not covet your neighbor's house. You shall not covet your neighbor's wife, or his male or female servant, his ox or donkey, or anything that belongs to your neighbor."

At some point in our lives, each of us can identify with a few commandments that we have disobeyed. As for me, I identify with several! But at some point, I realized I was tired–tired of both myself and my sins. I needed to repent, and I needed help. I needed help so that I could be delivered from my selfishness and from my sinful ways. I sat with My Father in Heaven and opened up the book of Genesis.

Although there are only a few chapters in Genesis that discuss Adam and Eve, they are packed with so much knowledge and revelation. In Genesis, God made it clear that He called man and woman to work together. Man was created to be the provider, and Woman was created to be his helpmeet.

However, the serpent Satan is always looking for ways to divide that relationship. He is cunning, calculating and is ALWAYS seeking to destroy the beauty of God's creation. And he definitely attempted to destroy the beauty of Adam and Eve's relationship with God and with each other.

So how do we beat Satan at His own game?! We can't, but God can! The only way to beat Satan is to fight him with the word of God.

Hebrews 4:12 (NIV) For the word of God is alive and active. Sharper than any double-edged sword, it penetrates even to dividing soul and spirit, joints and marrow; it judges the thoughts and attitudes of the heart.

We are called to meditate on the word of God daily. There is not one day on God's green Earth that passes where we don't need Him. We need God for His guidance, His instructions and His infinite wisdom. To paraphrase the old hymn, "We need Thee, every hour, we need Thee!"

I realized that if I wanted to succeed at love, I HAD to do it God's way! His way requires obedience.

When we are obedient to His laws, we walk alongside Him, and He can direct our paths towards the truth. He will expel from us the unclean spirits that are causing us to fail. We have to die to our old habits and allow God to create in us a clean heart, a heart like Jesus!

In order for us to succeed at love, we must become love. We must walk in love. We must walk WITH love **– Our Heavenly Father.**

Fundamental – What is your Vision?

We were created to help meet our husband's vision. However, the enemy's plan is for us to help distract him from his vision.

- **Felicia Ann**

Potential is not an indication of a man's purpose. Seek to align yourself with someone who chooses to align their vision after the heart of Jesus.

But blessed are your eyes because they see, and your ears because they hear. For truly I tell you, many prophets and righteous people longed to see what you see but did not see it, and to hear what you hear but did not hear it. **Matthew 13:16-17 (NIV)**

There is a God-born leader in both the male and the female. While your husband has the headship role, your leadership skills are equally as important under his headship. However, the fundamentals of your role can become exacerbated by lack of vision and the lack of the execution of that vision within your home.

The leadership role that you take on inside the home is a very important role. Think of yourself as the manager. Your role requires organization, leadership, effective communication, problem solving, goal setting, strategizing, budget management, as well as assisting with enforcing the house rules.

Managerial skills coincide with the title of helpmeet. Your husband has his vision for your home, and you have a vision for your home as well. Work to combine your God-given gifts to implement those visions and, if you should get distracted, refer back to the Creator of the vision to help each of you regain focus. **Joshua 24:15 (NIV) …But as for me and my household, we will serve the Lord."** The ultimate goal is to ensure that the vision is in alignment with what Our Heavenly Father loves. We are to build our homes with Jesus as our Chief Cornerstone **(Ephesians 2:20).**

Additionally, effectively managing the vision consists of instilling in our children the laws set forth by God. **Proverbs 22:6, (NIV) says, "Start children off on the way they should go, and even when they are old they will not turn from it."** We should strive to provide an extension of love to both our husband and our children. In addition, we should present ourselves as an example of God's love and light. Nurture the souls within our home with the Fruit of the Spirit. Implement God's commandments along with conjoining the vision to impose a solid foundation.

Seek to incorporate the vision so that God can provide His provision. It is not our plans, but the plans of God that will prevail. **Proverbs 16:9 (NIV) says, "humans plan their course, but the Lord establishes their steps."** God gives us the ideas needed to pursue the vision. However, we are to commit our ways to Him so that He can order our steps.

Thus, we are to start with a vision that will yield direction and order within the home. Strive to communicate with our husband as his helpmeet our plan to help him carry out that vision. Enact best practices. Share your heart with one another. Incorporate the Fruit of the Spirit daily to provide the strength needed to endure. We are to stand on one accord regarding the vision. **Ecclesiastes 4:12 (NIV), A cord of three strands is not quickly broken.**

Whatever you mismanage, you lose.

Dr. Myles Munroe

What, then, shall we say in response to these things? If God is for us, who can stand against us? **Romans 8:31 (NIV)**

Where there is no revelation, people cast off restraint; but blessed is the one who heeds wisdom's instruction. **Proverbs 29:18 (NIV)**

Fundamental – In the Beginning, God Established Marriage Roles

In the beginning (Genesis) God created man in His image. Adam was formed from the dust of the ground and Eve was created from one of Adam's ribs. They were created in the most supernatural way, and each was gifted with their own purpose based upon their God-given assigned gender roles.

After God created Adam, **Genesis 2:15** (NIV) says, **The Lord God took the man and put him in the Garden of Eden to work in it and take care of it.** God created man to labor through the work of his hands. Therefore, the man was created as the provider.

God determined that it was not good for man to be alone. Genesis 2:21-23 (NIV) So the Lord God caused the man to fall into a deep sleep; and while he was sleeping, he took one of the man's ribs and then closed up the place with flesh. Then the Lord God made a woman from the rib he had taken out of the man, and he brought her to the man. The man said,

> "This is now bone of my bones
> and flesh of my flesh;
> she shall be called 'woman,'
> for she was taken out of man."

God knew that each gender would need to work as a team in order to carry out His Kingdom's purpose. The woman was created to not only fill a void but to also labor in fulfilling daily responsibilities as the helpmeet. As women, we labor through childbirth; additionally, the woman also continues her laboring in the home as the nurturer and homemaker.

The woman is the homemaker because God has designed her role to be a keeper of the home. Titus 2:4-5 (NIV), says then they can urge the younger women to love their husbands and children, to be self-controlled and pure, to be busy at home, to be kind, and to be subject to their husbands, so that no one will malign the word of God.

In addition, both the man and woman were designed to unify in the most harmonious way with the understanding, acceptance, and respect that brings peace into the covenant of marriage. However, none of this is possible if we fail to listen and obey the instructions of God that are written within the Holy Bible.

Through additional instruction, God generously blessed Adam with the freedom to eat off of any tree in the Garden with the exception of the tree of knowledge of good and evil. These instructions had no ambiguity; therefore, Eve was also aware of the directive from God. As proof of her awareness, **Genesis 3:2-3 (NIV) says, The woman said to the serpent, "We may eat fruit from the trees in the garden, but God did say, "You must not eat fruit from the tree that is in the middle of the garden, and you must not touch it, or you will die."**

Adam and Eve's disobedience to God's directive was sin, described as "the forbidden fruit."

God gives us free will. Was the tree of good and evil placed in the middle of the Garden as a metaphorical representation of "choice"? The instructions commanded them to "not to touch the tree."

However, if we're honest, anything that we are told *not to touch*, somehow just seems to intensify our curiosity. When God gives instructions, we should remember that He knows what is best for us. We should choose to obey and not allow our curiosity to cause us to sin.

When God gave the instruction to not touch the tree, God was trying to protect Adam and Eve from the exposure to sin and evil that was out in the world. He wanted to keep humans pure and Holy so that we could continue to dwell amongst Him, under His covering and safety.

However, when we choose to disobey, our sins are a direct result of disobedience and there are consequences for those choices. Disobedience has warped the perfect plan that God created as the blueprint for us to follow for marriage.

As a result, there is discord in the dynamics of how things should work within the home. It is the sin that we have exposed ourselves to over the years that has thwarted our view. Nevertheless, the instructions provided from God remain the same. **Numbers 23:19** (NIV) says, **God is not human, that he should lie, not a human being, that he should change his mind. Does he speak and then not act? Does he promise and not fulfill?**

God has provided instructions within the Holy Bible to help us maneuver through any uncertainty. It is up to us to read and meditate on His word daily so that we can live the life that He promised us; we have to obey our Father in order to receive His best. It is only to our detriment when we choose to look beyond God's word and seek advice from a carnal view of how we should cohabitate. As a result, too often our flesh takes priority over our obedience, and we operate selfishly versus operating under the obedience of our Father.

When we reflect back to the garden, we see that once Adam and Eve committed sin, division began–division between Adam and Eve and, even worse, division between humans and God.

Adam blamed God for giving him Eve and Eve blamed the serpent for persuading her to eat from the tree. Adam neglected to take accountability and acknowledge that God only *presented* Eve to him and that *he* named her and called her "bone of my bone and flesh of my flesh!"

In addition, Adam did not take accountability for his failure to take responsibility as the head of the home and his wife. As the head of the home, he should have reiterated to Eve the instructions they were both given from God. As the head, who was seeking a directive on how to navigate through unfamiliar territory, his reliance on Our Heavenly Father was imperative.

Additionally, Eve also failed to accept accountability. Although she accurately repeated God's instructions to the serpent that she was *not to eat* from the tree of good and evil, she still failed to walk in obedience. Neither took accountability for their actions of disobedience or their individual failure to obey the laws from God.

God's instructions were only meant to provide a hedge of protection over the couple so that they would not encounter sin that would eventually lead to death. God was setting up the house rules as a display of His unconditional love for mankind. However, Adam and Eve were in direct violation of one of the ten commandments, "Honor your father and your mother, so that you may live long in the land the Lord your God is giving you." **Exodus 20:12** (NIV).

Fundamental – The Role of the Husband

Like Adam and Eve, sin has us second-guessing God's instructions and being disobedient to the laws that He has spoken in our present day and age. Although the blame game may achieve instant gratification for one's flesh, it is still wreaking havoc and causing division within marriages. We must remember that God established the order within the home.

Because the man is the head of the home, it is wise to take into consideration the man that you are choosing to marry. Choosing to submit to a man who is living outside of the will of God will result in confusion within your home.

1 Corinthians 7 highlights what it means to marry "in the Lord".

You should seek to yoke in covenant with a believer, who also shares your faith in Jesus Christ for his salvation.

Additionally, beyond belief, seek to embrace a man who understands his role as the provider, one who has a vision, a man who can help improve you both spiritually and mentally and one who is obedient to the word of God.

Equally important, your relationship with God will aid your resistance to fleshly desires that could lead to disobedience. While you are waiting to be found, take advantage of your singleness by strengthening your relationship with our Father so that you have the awareness to not be pursued by a spiritually immature man that is not after God's heart.

If you choose a man who is not seeking the presence of God, he will have a tough time understanding how to love you as Christ loves His church. Through his personal relationship with our Father, he can understand how to love because he chooses to receive instructions from the One who created love. Seek to embrace a spiritually mature man who is in step with God. Seek clarity through prayer and patience. Seek and trust our Father in Heaven, as there is no one here on Earth that can instruct us better than the one who knows us best; Our Creator-God!

Adam was given dominion over the animals and once he was presented with Eve, he became her covering as well. Therefore, being that man was created in God's image, he is capable of doing the work of the Lord. His obedience will cause the Holy Spirit to dwell within him and instruct him daily. Although Jesus is no longer walking the Earth in the flesh, we were left with his instructions on how to love as the ultimate Bridegroom loves.

Ephesians 5:25-29 (NIV) says, Husbands, love your wives, just as Christ loved the church and gave himself up for her to make her holy, cleansing her by the washing with water through the word, and to present her to himself as a radiant church, without stain or wrinkle or any other blemish, but holy and blameless. In this same way, husbands ought to love their wives as their own bodies. He who loves his wife loves himself. After all, no one ever hated their own body, but they feed and care for their body, just as Christ does the church–

Husbands have the obligation of loving and caring for their wives the same way they love and care for their own bodies, for to love your wife is to love your own self.

Ephesians 5:33 (NIV) says, However, each one of you also must love his wife as he loves himself, and the wife must respect her husband. In this letter, Paul tells husbands to love, provide and protect in the same manner that God is lovingly providing and protecting His church. When a wife feels provided for and protected, she feels loved. When a wife does not have to question her husband's character and trusts that her husband is faithful within his covenant with God, she is free to fill her role as the nurturing helpmeet that God created her to be. A man's faithfulness to God is a reflection of his commitment to her.

According to **Genesis 2:24 (NIV), That is why a man leaves his father and mother and is united to his wife, and they become one flesh.** When a man and woman decide to marry, they leave the protection and covering of their parents or guardian and they both cleave to one another to create a covering of love and protection within their own home. As the head, the husband receives his vision and instructions from God. He shares his vision with his wife. His wife helps him with his vision.

Fundamental – God is the Head of the Home

That is why a man leaves his father and mother and is united to his wife, and they become one flesh. **Genesis 2:24 (NIV)**

This scripture highlights how a man leaves the covering of his father's home and joins his wife within the home that they establish together after marriage. According to the Bible, God created Adam first and then created Eve as his helpmeet. The man is the head of his home, and he is to seek his guidance from the Godhead, which consists of God the Father, Jesus Christ, and the Holy Spirit.

Most importantly, God is the head over the entire home. Therefore, both the husband and wife should have a personal relationship with God so that they can seek Him individually for the knowledge, wisdom and discernment of how to unify to create the structure that God requires them to establish for their household. All direction should come from Our Heavenly Father through the prayers of both the wife and the husband. The prayers not only help to mitigate chaos and confusion within the home, but it creates a unified front. This is the way God intended life to be lived within the marital covenant, as one flesh under His supervision.

Let's face it, no one is born with the knowledge of how to be a wife. However, with the guidance from our Father in Heaven, we can become a Godly one. We can become the Godly wife that God created Eve to be prior to the fall of mankind. We can help our husband within our home while he goes out to labor for his family.

We can learn how to submit to our husband the way that God intended.

Ephesians 5:21 (NIV) says, Submit to one another out of reverence for Christ.

Submission does not mean that you are incapable of making decisions or that you lose your voice within the home.

Godly submission establishes order within the home so that the home can remain peaceful and manageable. A submitting wife trusts her husband's decision-making, even if there are times when she is unsure if he is making the right decision. She should pray that his relationship with God will lead him in the right direction.

1 Corinthians 11:3 (NIV) says, But I want you to realize that the head of every man is Christ, and the head of the woman is man, and the head of Christ is God.

God established order within the marital home. As believers in God, we should understand that everything God creates has order. God's laws were created to establish order on Earth. Without order, confusion will ensue. Being that Satan dwells amongst confusion, choosing to follow order can minimize disorder. Thus, it is very important to marry a man who is after God's heart.

2 Corinthians 6:14 (NIV) instructs, Do not be yoked together with unbelievers. For what do righteousness and wickedness have in common? Or what fellowship can light have with darkness?

As the head of the family, the husband is instructed to seek God and to remain faithful and obedient. The wife is to submit to the husband.

Submission does not imply militant conforming. However, it allows the husband to make the final decisions if there is any discrepancy between the husband and wife. The husband should be willing to assume accountability in the event that his decision does not have a favorable outcome. Allow room for grace and forgiveness because the Holy Spirit has already acted on our behalf and set the standard.

Ephesians 5:22-23 (NIV) says, Wives, submit to your own husbands as you do to the Lord. For the husband is the head of the wife as Christ is the head of the church, his body, of which he is the Savior.

Husbands were created to be the head of the house and reflect God's love. A man who is seeking instructions from God creates the submissive nature within the wife. Her submissive nature reflects respect towards her husband.

When a woman submits respectfully to her husband, this is a display of love. A man who has integrity, works hard to provide for his family, and seeks God for His vision, direction and understanding, deserves respect. Respectfully, wives should trust that along with God's guidance, the husband can and will make wise decisions concerning his family. Needless to say, if he should fail to do so, nurture his efforts with prayer and encouragement that he continues seeking God for clarity.

Colossians 3:18-19 (NIV) says, Wives, submit yourselves to your husbands, as is fitting in the Lord. Husbands, love your wives and do not be harsh with them.

Just as wives are to submit to their husbands, God has instructed husbands not to be harsh with their wives. As a wife, please know that through self-love, you can recognize manipulative, counterfeit, and toxic behavior. You shouldn't allow someone to degrade you with their abusive and cruel words, cheating behavior or personal insecurities. No one should cause you mental anguish or setbacks as you continue to seek God to heal and become the wife that He created you to be. It is important to recognize unhealthy behavior and recognize how you should be loved according to God's word.

It is equally important that you love with a heart that is pleasing to God and not reflect unhealthy emotions onto your husband. Never ignore warning signs and forgo your peace in an attempt to gain temporary happiness. Stay steadfast and trust God to allow you to experience His love through the man that He has for you. Allow God to work on the areas where you may have lacked love growing up so that you can distinguish pragma-enduring love vs limerence love. Choose to wait and be patient with the time that it takes for love to blossom. Choose to not settle for the frills of the display of love and choose to seek love that is created through a Godly foundation.

Fundamental – The Bible Defines Marriage as a Covenant

Prior to choosing to enter into a marriage covenant, we were born into a covenant with God. First, we should seek to understand what is required of us as believers to be under the blood covenant with our Father in Heaven. Under God's covenant with Abraham, God offered His protection and land to Abraham and his descendants. As a descendant of Abraham, we are required to be obedient to the word of God in order to inhabit the Promise Land.

God suffered and died on the cross for our sins. In doing so, He made promises through His death and the shedding of His blood on the cross. The crucifixion of Christ was *love in its purest form.*

Matthew 26:28 (NIV) says, This is my blood of the covenant, which is poured out for many for the forgiveness of sins.

Being in covenant with God requires our faithfulness to Him. We are to trust God for His provision, His protection and His faithfulness to us and our overall well-being. We are to walk in love with God daily and ask Him to guide and teach us through the Holy Spirit how to become a Godly wife.

Malachi 2:14, (NIV) describes marriage as a holy covenant before God. ...she is your partner, the wife of your marriage covenant.

Additionally, we should seek how to use our gifts and talents within our home to help our husband and rear our child(ren).

Anything that we can and will struggle with, God has a solution that can be found within the Holy Bible.

Fundamental – God Hates Divorce

God is against anything that could lead to divorce and requires that we remain faithful to one another. **Exodus 20:14 (NIV), is the 7th commandment, and states You shall not commit adultery.**

This rule is echoed in Matthew 5:27 (NIV). You have heard that it was said, 'You shall not commit adultery.'

We are to obey our Father's laws and resist the temptation to covet any other man once we are in covenant with our husband. As a wife, it is a requirement that we remain faithful to our husband. Likewise, it is a requirement that our husband also remains faithful to us. We are to forsake all others and be faithful by encouraging, supporting and trusting our husband in his decision-making for our home.

This law addresses adulterous relationships and encompasses both physical and emotional sin.

The same desires of faithfulness that we seek from our husband, God also seeks from us. Being in covenant with God requires our faithfulness to Him. We are to walk in love with God daily and ask Him to guide and teach us through the Holy Spirit how to serve Him through our good works and by spreading the good news.

Knowing the affliction that Jesus suffered for our sins and His abundance of love and mercy, we should seek to understand the severity of what it means to be in and to remain in covenant with

God. By recognizing the seriousness of what it means to be in covenant with our Father in Heaven, you gain an understanding of what it means to commit to a covenant with your husband.

God will forever be faithful and never forsake you. This is His promise and commitment to His church. When you enter into a covenant with God, you are required to forsake all others, which includes the worshiping of idols or anything other than Him. This includes the things that keep us distracted from spending time in His Holy presence. The Holy Bible is aware that idolatry can extend beyond worshiping images and false gods. Idolization can come in the form of greed, gluttony, pride, self-centeredness and anything that relates to matters of the heart that are not solely focused on our Father in Heaven.

Additionally, we should not put anything or anyone before God. We show our commitment to God by prioritizing Him. Idolization is also forbidden for our husband. We should love our husband with all of our heart. However, we should only worship our Father in Heaven and love Him with all of our heart, mind and soul (Matthew 22:37-40).

Our faithfulness to God is a prerequisite of our faithfulness to the covenant that we are seeking with our husband. A wife's faithfulness to her husband is a commandment within the covenant of marriage. More importantly, it is also required within our covenant with Jesus Christ. Therefore, seek God for clarification of what it means to be in blood covenant with Him. As you seek Him, you will gain a clearer understanding of what God requires to be within the holy sanctity of the covenant of marriage as well.

God requires us to be an obedient and faithful servant. He requires that we seek Him above all. Matthew 6:33 (NIV) says, But seek first his kingdom and his righteousness, and all these things will be given to you as well.

Seeking God and His righteousness comes with rewards. Once we seek to know the unknown and to build our relationship with our Heavenly Father; He sees our heart, our obedience, and dedication, and rewards our effort. He rewards us with His everlasting promises. His rewards extend beyond tangible items, such as money, houses and cars. His rewards are peace that surpasses all understanding and unspeakable joy. His rewards are priceless jewels that only He can give!

One of his rewards is our ability to experience His fruit through His Spirit. Those fruits are love, joy, patience, kindness, goodness, gentleness, self-control, forgiveness and faithfulness. He gives us a blessed assurance that He is ours and that no matter what issues we face, He is more than able to see us through. His covenant guides, protects and keeps us safe.

Ephesians 5:25-27, (NIV) says, Husbands, love your wives, just as Christ loved the church and gave himself up for her to make her holy, cleansing her by the washing with water through the word, and to present her to himself as a radiant church, without stain or wrinkle or any other blemish, but holy and blameless.

This scriptural text provides context of how God loves us and expects the husband, who is the head of the home, to also love his wife.

Seek to understand the reason that God hates divorce before you agree to the covenant of marriage. Matthew 19:3-10 (NIV) says, Some Pharisees came to him to test him. They asked, "Is it lawful for a man to divorce his wife for any and every reason?" "Haven't you read," he replied, "that at the beginning the Creator 'made them male and female,' and said, 'For this reason a man will leave his father and mother and be united to his wife, and the two will become one flesh'? So, they are no longer two, but one flesh. Therefore, what God has joined together, let no one separate." "Why then," they asked, "did Moses command that a man give his wife a certificate of divorce and send her away?" Jesus replied, "Moses permitted you to divorce your wives because your hearts were hard. But it was not this way from the beginning. I tell you that anyone who divorces his wife, except for sexual immorality, and marries another woman commits adultery." The disciples said to him, "If this is the situation between a husband and wife, it is better not to marry."

Spend time with our Heavenly Father so that you don't disappoint Him. Make the commitment to keep your vows and obey God's instructions. Do not succumb to your fleshly desires.

Fruit of the Spirit – God Is Our Spiritual Fruit Basket

Imagine a fruit basket filled with the ripest, most nutritious, and delicious fruits. Each one carries substance and is packed with an immeasurable amount of all the vitamins and energy you need to live. Imagine that each fruit could help you to combat and eliminate the stress and worry of your everyday life.

Now imagine that these fruits don't have to be prepared, eaten or digested because the nutrients from these fruits are flowing within you daily. Also, they are available at no cost to you. The only requirement is that you seek the Holy Spirit daily to obtain them.

Acts 2:38 (NIV) "Repent and be baptized, every one of you, in the name of Jesus Christ for the forgiveness of your sins. And you will receive the gift of the Holy Spirit."

This is the amazing – and bountiful – gift that God gave us with the Fruit of the Holy Spirit.

Galatians 5:22-23 (NIV) says "But the fruit of the Spirit is love, joy, peace, forbearance, kindness, goodness, faithfulness, gentleness and self-control. Against such things there is no law."

You simply grow your relationship with Him and He waters you within to create an abundant harvest. Imagine having a lifetime supply of everything that you need to function abundantly in every area of your life. What a beautiful gift basket!

Fruit of the Spirit – Love

God's love is so delightful-any other pleasure seems dismal in comparison with it.

- **St. Catherine of Genoa**

Love is a force more formidable than any other. It is invisible-it cannot be seen or measured, yet it is powerful enough to transform you in a moment and offer you more joy than any material possession could.

- **Barbara De Angelis**

God is love. Our first Love is God. No one can teach us how to love better than the one who is love itself.

Love is sacrificial. We are called to first, "Love the Lord your God with all your heart and with all your soul and with all your mind." Matthew 22:37 (NIV).

When you choose your spouse, there is still work to be done. You are not made whole through the covenant of marriage alone. You are to become one by choosing to wash each other daily through the love of God. **Genesis 2:24** (NIV) says, That is why a man leaves his father and mother and is united to his wife, and they become one flesh.

We must engage in an intimate relationship with our Father in Heaven. He loves us so much and He supplies all of our needs. He is the source of our daily bread and without Biblical scriptures, we will become malnourished.

Through His living word, God will begin to work on your heart and transform you. As He transforms and transplants in you a new heart, it is being prepared to receive love and to give love. He can also expose any misconceptions that you may have about love. As a result, you can now understand what love looks like through our Heavenly Father's eyes.

The way that our Father loves us prepares us to understand how God instructed a husband to love his wife and a wife to love her husband. God gives us unconditional love.

1 Corinthians 13:4-7 (NIV), Love is patient, love is kind. It does not envy, it does not boast, it is not proud. It does not dishonor others, it is not self-seeking, it is not easily angered, and it keeps no record of wrongs. Love does not delight in evil but rejoices with the truth. It always protects, always trusts, always hopes, always perseveres.

Love has patience when we are trying to overcome hurt and disappointment. Love does not become easily angered or resentful. Love doesn't bring up past mistakes and look for a way to make the other person feel bad through calloused words. Love is a fruit that bears good seed that can multiply an abundant harvest if watered correctly.

God requires the husband to love His wife in the same manner that He loves the entire body of Christ. He requires the husband to love His wife based upon God's Biblical instructions. This is why it is important to yoke with a man who desires the presence of the Lord, who is dedicated to spending quality time with the Lord daily and is obedient to God's word. In doing so, the husband will understand just how to love his wife through reading and meditating on the word.

The husband has the role to provide and protect his wife and to be willing to sacrifice all for her just as God did for the entire body of Christ when He was brutally slain on the cross. There is a sense of security that embodies a woman knowing that her husband is protecting and covering her not only physically and financially but, most importantly, spiritually.

Additionally, a woman feels emotionally secure knowing that she can rely on her husband to seek God, and, as a result, she safely submits to her husband and trusts in his provision for their home. Although women are capable of financially contributing to the household as well, our hearts are empowered with love knowing and trusting that our husband has the integrity to financially be the provider for our home.

In Genesis, God created Adam as the provider. This is an example of one of God's standard operating procedures within the home. Through the understanding of our role as the helpmeet, the recourse from our husband for financial protection allows us to lovingly submit to the order set forth by our Heavenly Father. Our husband's role as provider creates a deeper love within us. Admiring our husband's desire to make sure that his wife and children are truly taken care of provides an internal high regard of appreciation.

Through intimate time with God, He can teach you what love truly means, how to love yourself and how to love your husband or future husband. He will teach you how to incorporate the Fruit of the Spirit into marriage.

Therefore, you can recognize if the man you are considering as a future husband is truly a man after God's heart. Through the help of the Holy Spirit, God will heighten your discernment and wisdom while in your season of preparation.

We all desire to have love, to feel love and to be loved. God's love is not selfish; rather, it is life-affirming, sacrificial, and endless. **John 3:16 (NIV), For God so loved the world that he gave his one and only Son, that whoever believes in him shall not perish but have eternal life.**

In our fleshly bodies, it is hard to give without expecting something in return. Once we share our love, if we don't feel that love reciprocated, we tend to express our disappointment through anger, resentment, slander or simply internalize our disappointment. As a result, we may vow to never love again!

This is not pleasing to God. Throughout the Bible, God shows us time and time again to consistently show love. Reading His word and building an intimate relationship with our Father in Heaven, will teach us how to not be afraid to love.

Loving God first and then ourselves is essential to loving others. Don't miss out on God's best because of failure to do the hard work. Choose to seek God so that He can introduce you to His love and understanding. If love is what you are truly seeking as a desire within your heart, stay committed to doing it God's way and He will steer you through those bumpy roads.

Ask God how to genuinely love within your role as a helpmeet. In the Bible, three women that sat with Jesus are examples of women serving as a helpmeet. Each of them had the name Mary: Mary, Jesus' mother, Lazarus' sister Mary of Bethany, and Mary Magdalene, who Jesus sent to spread the good news that He had risen from the dead.

Each of these women are so inspiring. They had an individual and collective love of Jesus. Each of them sat ever so patiently at Jesus' feet with admiration and with a heart of pure love.

The role of the woman is very important. As nurturers, we have the ability to love in a way that is inviting and comforting. Our love has the ability to provide calmness and reassurance. The role of a wife is not to be taken lightly. We are to uplift, encourage and support our husband. It is an important role that requires dedication and patience. Through our encouragement, we can help our husband to walk in his Godly purpose.

Pray and ask God to help you to not mismanage your love. As you prepare, don't waste your time and effort with a man that is not creating the time or putting forth the effort to engage enough to get to know you. God will help you recognize who is good for YOU so that together the two of you can become Kingdom driven to spread the good news.

In addition, you both can pour the love of Jesus into your family and into your community.

Trust God and trust His process. He is a loving Father who will not fail you. He will hold your hand and walk you through the insight of what a loving relationship looks like. You cannot forfeit this process if you want to love God's way.

Remember, you are preparing to become a wife for the man that He has prepared for YOU. The things that God is teaching you and your personal journey may not be the teachings or journey that He is providing for someone else. We all have our own unique journey. The Father is creating a great work in you so that you can experience a boundless love.

Titus 3:4-7 (NIV) But when the kindness and love of God our Savior appeared, he saved us, not because of righteous things we had done, but because of his mercy. He saved us through the washing of rebirth and renewal by the Holy Spirit, whom he poured out on us generously through Jesus Christ our Savior, so that, having been justified by his grace, we might become heirs having the hope of eternal life.

Choosing to love God's way will reap rewards. Choosing to love requires us to surrender and trust in a way that leaves us vulnerable. We have to be open to forgiveness and possible disappointments that come along with seeking love from our husband. Because we can only control our actions and not the actions of another individual, choose to put your hope and trust in God and allow Him to guide you and give the necessary protection for your heart. Trust God to teach you how to love the man that He chooses to present you to as a helpmeet and choose to love without limits.

As beautiful as the idea of love is, you risk a few wounds along the way. The wounds become scars that can testify to your willingness to battle through some treacherous conditions. Your wounds create strength and endurance that could lead to your happily ever after.

Thank God that He meets us right where we are and walks with us. What a privilege it is to have God's patience and kindness to teach us the mystery of love. God exclaims His love for us in the Bible 310 times in 280 verses. There are so many scriptures He gave to teach us about love and how to express love. Take time to impart love into your heart so that you can truly learn how to love and how to be receptive to the gift of love.

Keep yourselves in God's love as you wait for the mercy of our Lord Jesus Christ to bring you to eternal life. **Jude 1:21 (NIV).**

Love did not hurt you, someone who didn't know how to love hurt you.

- **Tony Gaskins**

Prayer:

Dear Heavenly Father,

As I seek to understand love, help guide me with Your wisdom and knowledge. Help me to give love that is not selfish, boastful or jealous. I desire to openly give love and receive love that is pleasing to You. As I continue to grow, I ask that You help me recognize when I am loving in a way that is not pleasing to You. Thank You for your agape love and the patience to reshape my mind for the former ways where I misunderstood love. I love that You created me to love and I desire to experience a boundless love. In Jesus' name, amen!

The first question you ask a man who is interested in you, is not do you love me; …. but do you love God's presence.

- Dr. Myles Munroe

Fruit of the Spirit – Joy

Joy is a net of Love by which you can catch souls…We can do no great things-only small things with great love.

- **Mother Teresa**

To be simply ensconced in God is true joy.

- **C.C. Colton**

BE JOYFUL! The Bible tells us to be joyful multiple times.

Satisfy us in the morning with your unfailing love, that we may sing for joy and be glad all our days. **Psalm 90:14 (NIV)**

I have told you this so that my joy may be in you and that your joy may be complete. **John 15:11 (NIV)**

There is no greater feeling than the joy that the Lord brings to your heart. It is a feeling that is truly indescribable. The joy of the Lord erases the heavy and unfulfilled feelings brought by the burdens of life.

So how can we obtain this joy so that we can overcome the feeling that our burdens bring upon us?

Daily talks with God help to overshadow those unwanted feelings. Dedicate yourself to a daily routine of alone time with God and allowing Him to cover you in His armor, which is the scripture within the Holy Bible. This is a requirement to get through all of the things that life can throw at any given moment.

The saying "the best things in life are free" is so true when it comes to the Fruit of the Spirit - especially joy! God's salvation, grace, and mercy are free to His followers. These precious jewels cost us absolutely nothing! We can't swipe our credit cards to purchase them; it's our time with our precious Lord and Savior that becomes currency.

Sitting quietly and waiting for the Lord to come into your heart, mind and soul will bring a happiness that moves one to tears. He will fill you up in ways that you never knew you needed. Don't be surprised if He makes you feel giddy! There's a spirit of excitement – of joy – when you link up with the Father to help you persevere through any and all adversity that you will face.

Once you feel joy in your heart, you long for it and you understand just how valuable it is. That type of joy does not come from anyone else other than our Savior.

Therefore, if you are looking for your husband to give you joy, I encourage you to first seek the supernatural feeling of joy that is provided from the Holy Spirit that God placed inside of us. It will give you comfort when you are feeling alone and vulnerable. His joy will fill the emptiness and hug you ever so tightly. Prayerfully, this will become an infectious energy that will attract our husbands and others to desire to seek this feeling of joy through Christ as well.

As a helpmeet, our attitudes are a reflection of our Creator. Remember that we should not provoke but carry a softness that entices and captivates the reason that God created us to be a helpmeet. Allow the joy of the Lord to be your strength to endure adversity and be a representation of the goodness of the Lord.

If we have the joy of the Lord within us, we can cause a chain reaction for joy to flow within our marriage. Practice ways to stay joyful when things don't go as planned or you are in conflict. Seek the Lord for understanding on how to create joy within so that you may also create joy within your home. Allow joy to transpose any feelings of ill will or unwarranted feelings so that you can bring peace and love.

You are truly in control of how you choose to react and respond to negativity. Choose to put joy on full display so that God's glory is on full display. **Deuteronomy 28:47-48** (NIV) says, **"Because you did not serve the Lord your God joyfully and gladly in the time of prosperity, therefore in hunger and thirst, in nakedness and dire poverty, you will serve the enemies the Lord sends against you. He will put an iron yoke on your neck until he has destroyed you.**

Do not depend upon your own strength to create joy; you lack the ability to have it without God. Nothing is possible without Him. Choose to serve God and allow His joy to abound within you. Take time to quiet yourself and invite the Holy Spirit to come into your heart and mind to provide joy. Allow the Holy Spirit to set the atmosphere and encompass his love through you. Stay in the secret place with Him until His joy arrests you. Whatever you need, seek God and keep seeking His face for His immeasurable joy!

"...This day is holy to our Lord. Do not grieve, for the joy of the Lord is your strength." Nehemiah 8:10 (NIV)

I Though you have not seen him, you love him; and even though you do not see him now, you believe in him and are filled with an inexpressible and glorious joy, for you are receiving the end result of your faith, the salvation of your souls. 1 Peter 1:8-9 (NIV)

Prayer:

Dear God,

Create in me the joy that only You can. Allow joy to flow through me as a representation of Your glory. Allow my joy to be infectious so that I can be a living example of the true joy that loving You brings. Allow me to understand how to have joy during the times when I am not in a joyous place. Increase my discernment of how to obtain joy and how to spread joy. In Jesus' name, amen!

Fruit of the Spirit – Peace

Peace is the awesome gift of God given to those who surrender their ways and walk in His will.

- **Pastor Jody Ray**

Peace I leave with you; my peace I give you. I do not give to you as the world gives. Do not let your hearts be troubled and do not be afraid. **John 14:27** (NIV)

You've heard the saying, Peace is priceless! Yes, without a doubt. Peace is truly something that trumps any other feeling.

True peace is found in God. When you have peace from the Lord, you have an internal knowing that provides assurance that everything will work for good.

Peace is a choice. If you choose to surrender control and make peace with knowing that God has full control of absolutely everything that transpires in His Earth, you will allow God's perfect will to be done worry free. When you surrender and recognize God's hand at work in your life, no matter the circumstance, you can trust that He only wants the best for you.

However, in order to surrender and trust Him, you must stay steadfast and endure the process of relationship-building with our Father. Trust that everything will work out in your favor because He is the one true living God. God is sovereign and omnipresent.

Desire to create a peaceful life within your home. Moreover, in order to obtain peace, you have to seek peace from the Prince of Peace. Remember God is the vine, and we are the branches. He has to prune us and cut things from us things that are not of Him. We all have things inside of us that can disturb our peace or create a not so peaceful environment for others. We cannot do this alone. Make peace with God through supplication.

Next, focus on making peace with yourself. If there are any areas that you have denied God access into, allow Him to enter in and begin healing those areas of hurt and disappointment. Unfortunately, we have all experienced trauma in our lives at some point. Refusing to acknowledge the trauma and suppressing it does not make it disappear. You have to deal with the issue(s) and ask God to release any strongholds that are prevalent in your life.

Through God's power, you can seek peace by dissolving as much hurt from your heart as you possibly can. Choosing not to make peace with yourself will only cause flare ups in relationships. These flare ups may include trust issues, anger and insecurities. Cast out the spirit of offense and instead seek to find peace. Seek to find healing for what offended you and practice self-control so that you can usher peace in that area.

You deserve to experience the healed version of yourself.

You deserve to create a home inside of your heart that welcomes the true goodness that only God's peace can bring.

Once you focus on peace with God and yourself, you can focus on peace with others. Don't allow unforgiveness to take your peace. Refuse to hold on to any disturbing thoughts or feelings that come to mind when you think of any ill intent that was done to you. Instead, choose peace. Choose to let go of any misunderstandings, wrongdoings and toxic behaviors that have created an unhealthy mindset. Take those offenses to God and lay them at his feet; ask Him to help you overcome them.

The peace of God will transition into how you handle offenses within your home. Additionally, your preparation will help you to manage the offenses that your spouse may present to you. Prepare for peace!

Prayer:

Dear God,

Help me prepare for peace. As I seek you, the Prince of Peace, show me what true peace feels like and how to maintain it. Please help me to desire peace so that when the storms of life try to overpower my mental capacity, your peace will sustain me, reassuring me with the knowledge that You are in full control. Help me to overflow with peace so that others see and desire to seek Your peace as well. Allow me to create a home of peace and not of worry or strife. Thank you, God, for being my Prince of Peace, and Jehovah Shalom. In Jesus' name, amen!!

Isaiah 54:10 (NIV) "Though the mountains be shaken and the hills removed, yet my unfailing love for you will not be shaken nor my covenant of peace be removed," says the Lord, who has compassion on you.

Fruit of the Spirit – Kindness

A warm smile is the universal language of kindness.

- **William Arthur Ward**

Be kind and compassionate to one another, forgiving each other, just as in Christ God forgave you. **Ephesians 4:32 (NIV)**

Kindness is selfless, compassionate, and merciful. Kindness is choosing to display compassion versus choosing to react out of agitation.

He has shown you, O mortal, what is good. And what does the Lord require of you? To act justly and to love mercy and to walk humbly with your God. **Micah 6:8 (NIV)**

When we choose to love someone, we incorporate kindness. We are wise with the words we speak, and we understand how to tame our tongue from spewing out unkind words. We choose to follow Jesus and mimic the way that He treats us and how He chooses to respond to us when He is not pleased with our actions. Jesus provided the examples of how we should respond within the covenant that we made with our husband.

A combative tone or a snappy response will not trigger a loving response from your husband. Be mindful that the reaction that you give could in turn provide the same response that was given. Choose kindness. Choose to take a step back from reacting in a way that satisfies your flesh. Choose to consult our Father in Heaven and seek His advice on how to kindly handle any situation that could result in an irritable response.

Don't feel pressured to react in the moment. Choose to take a moment to collect yourself so that you can respond with kindness. Don't allow the enemy to cause strife within your home because you are choosing to give an unkind response. Walk away, breathe and pray.

When you choose the fruit of kindness, you will reap the same kind of fruit from your husband. Luke 6:38 (NIV) says; Give, and it will be given to you. A good measure, pressed down, shaken together, and running over, will be poured into your lap. For with the measure you use, it will be measured to you.

Focus on the long-term goal of how your kind words and responses can harvest goodness and mercy in your life. Focus on how kindness will impact your marriage and the intimacy with your husband. When you are kind to one another, you connect on a more compassionate, intimate level. You create an intimate connection that brings forth love, which manifests into a spirit of servitude. You submit to one another with love and kindness as an expression of respect. Your kind spirit will foster a reciprocation of the goodness of God. Don't respond irrationally, respond with love…respond with kindness!

A gentle answer turns away wrath, but a harsh word stirs up anger. The tongue of the wise adorns knowledge, but the mouth of the fool gushes folly. **Proverbs 15:1-2** (NIV)

Prayer:

Dear Heavenly Father,

Help me to bear the fruit of kindness. Teach me how to tame my tongue from spewing out words that can lead to strife. Teach me how to lean on the Holy Spirit to direct me with my decisions to create a gentle answer. Allow Your kindness to manifest inside of me so that I am a living example of how You have been ever so kind to me and the entire body of Christ, although we are undeserving. Continue to teach me Your ways and forgive me for having the spirit of offense that has caused me to act out in a way that is not pleasing to You. In Jesus' name, amen!

Fruit of the Spirit – Goodness

Nothing good exists outside of God's presence.

- **Felicia Dance**

I remain confident of this: I will see the goodness of the Lord in the land of the living. Wait for the Lord; be strong and take heart and wait for the Lord. **Psalm 27:13-14 (NIV)**

God is the ultimate essence of goodness. God alone is good!

Goodness is a natural reflection of the Fruit of the Spirit at work in our life. It is an outward reflection of an inward change. God's fruit overpowers the sinful nature that lies inside of humanity. Therefore, it is impossible to obtain this fruit unless you are truly committed to the Lord and committed to a renewed heart. The action behind goodness is a pureness that uplifts and sustains you.

If you desire a marriage that provides goodness, it is only found through the Lord. God's goodness is present in the fullness of the Spirit; His Spirit can be found near and far. If you seek to find God, you will find His goodness!

Lamentations 3:25 (NIV) says, **The Lord is good to those whose hope is in him, to the one who seeks him.** When we seek the Lord, we are seeking His goodness. If we are not seeking the Lord, we begin to innately seek self-righteousness.

Marriage is a selfless union. If we truly desire a good marriage, we have to seek God and ask Him to bind the selfishness that each of us possess. We should strive to have God's glory revealed through us so that we can become a reflection of His goodness within our respective unions.

We have to believe that God is more than capable of meeting our marital needs. We have to know that God's goodness covers every area in our lives. We have to ask God for His goodness and mercy to manifest within our marriage. We need more of Him and less of us!

As conduits of God's living water that flows within us, recognize that His goodness overpowers any hardships that we may face. As a representation of Christ, we should choose to have the goodness of God flowing within us each and every day. We should choose to follow the example of how Jesus chose to show His goodness and mercy to an undeserving world.

Thinking of the goodness of God, you should seek to pour into your husband in the exact way that Jesus chooses to pour into us. When things don't go your way, God is still good, and His goodness still prevails. When we choose God, we choose His GOODNESS! Allow God's goodness to overtake you.

Where can I go from your Spirit? Where can I flee from your presence? If I go up to the heavens, you are there; if I make my bed in the depths, you are there. If I rise on the wings of the dawn, if I settle on the far side of the sea, even there your hand will guide me, your right hand will hold me fast. **Psalm 139:7-10 (NIV)**

Prayer:

Dear Heavenly Father,

Help me to choose goodness. I know that there may be days when I don't display the best attitude but help me to gather my thoughts to display goodness. Help me to become a reflection of your goodness by putting aside my feelings and choosing to be good. Help me to choose to show love, kindness and goodness daily.

Remind me of the many, many times that You have been so good to me when I didn't deserve Your goodness. As a result, I too should willingly spread goodness to others. In Jesus' name, amen!

Fruit of the Spirit – Forbearance

Only God can change the heart of a human being; but that human being has to have it in their heart to truly want to change.

- **Felicia Ann**

Forgiveness is not just words that we utter, but it is a true removal of the offense from our heart.

We often desire to be forgiven for the offense that we rendered; however, we tend to struggle with true forgiveness towards others. The Lord's prayer (**Matthew 6:9-13**) reminds us by saying, "Lord, forgive us of our trespasses, as we forgive those who trespass against us".

Ephesians 4:32 says, "Be kind to one another, tenderhearted, forgiving one another, as God in Christ forgave you."

Forgiveness is not one sided. We cannot require forgiveness from God or from others if we are unwilling to apply this Biblical principle as well. Ask God to search your heart to free you from the stronghold of resentment and anger that lack of forgiveness causes you. Desire to forgive as God forgives. Seek out all of the things that trigger bitterness and a scolded heart of resentment. Ask God to help you reflect on the circumstances that may have led another person to treat you poorly. Although you may have had nothing to do with the targeted offense, through prayer, ask God to help you have empathy for the person that offended you. Additionally, ask God to help them see how that person has hurt you. This way, if the opportunity presents itself for you to be able to talk through the offense, you will be able to clear up any misunderstandings with His patience and kindness.

God is pleased when we seek to forgive others. Remember that you are in covenant with God; therefore, what pleases God is the path of obedience that we should allow our hearts to follow. **Colossians 3:13 (NIV) "Bear with each other and forgive one another if any of you has a grievance against someone. Forgive as the Lord forgave you."**

Although most of humanity tends to hold on to the pain of mistreatment, we have to consider how God forgives us our sinful nature over and over and over again. It is pleasing to God when we turn to Him for help in forgiving and begin to trust in Him to heal the brokenness within.

Refuse to allow hurt to steal your peace and your joy. Surrender it over to God and allow Him to deal with it in whatever suitable way He chooses. It's not our battle to fight, it is God's. Focus instead on what we can control, which is the fight to remove the offense from our heart and choose to forgive.

Be mindful of the things that you say because words cannot be taken back. Refrain from saying hurtful things and hurling accusations without taking a moment to rest in your thoughts and respond with gentleness. Words can cause scarring within our minds, hearts and spirit. Be mindful of the things that you do that could be detrimental to others. Always remember to act and respond with love.

Matthew 6:14 (NIV) For if you forgive other people when they sin against you, your heavenly Father will also forgive you. But if you do not forgive others their sins, your Father will not forgive your sins. The Fruit of the Spirit should not only be displayed through our actions but should also be the fruit of how we handle tough conversations and respond to unwarranted accusations. Allow your words to speak life. Your conversation should not lead others to have trepidation. Invite the Holy Spirit to lead you and to guide you to effective and loving communication.

Forgiveness means that you sincerely, from the heart, cancel the other person's debt against you personally. Remember that we should forgive so that we can reconcile and no longer count our offenses against one another.

Throughout the duration of your marriage, forgiveness is mandatory. You will be both the offender and the offended. Countless times you will ask for forgiveness and be asked to forgive.

Matthew 18: 21-22 (NIV) Then Peter came to Jesus and asked, "Lord, how many times shall I forgive my brother or sister who sins against me? Up to seven times?" Jesus answered, "I tell you, not seven times, but seventy-seven times."

As you prepare for marriage, work on strategies that promote open communication. Search for ways that you and your husband are able to openly discuss your feelings. If we choose to suppress our feelings, this can only lead to resentment. Each passing day that you hold on to the offense, you allow Satan to enter into your mind to implant false accusations of the offender. **Ephesians 4:26 (NIV) "In your anger do not sin." Do not let the sun go down while you are still angry.**

Once the sun goes down and darkness takes over, the enemy has the opportunity to run rampant. Satan implants strife and this can only spiral into more and more resentment, which can cause you to become more enraged. Through our desire to forgive, God gets the glory.

Allow forgiveness to be your therapy for healing your brokenness.

Forgiveness doesn't mean that the offender gets away with the offense. However, it mentally and spiritually frees you of the hurt from the offense. Through forgiveness, you allow yourself to gain control from the emotional turmoil, and you are able to move forward with love.

Once you search deep within to remove the anger and resentment, God can work to circumcise your heart. Forgiveness doesn't always lead to reconciliation. However, forgiveness gives you peace of mind. This in turn allows you the possibility of peaceful reconciliation. With forgiveness, you are free from the heaviness of resentment and anger. Choose to forgive the offender.

Prayer:

Dear Heavenly Father,

Help me to forgive, just as you have graciously forgiven me time and time again. Help me to not allow the offense to manifest into resentment. Help me to resolve the conflict that leads to unforgiveness with patience and kindness. Guide me to see the offense the same way that you see my offenses and lead me to respond with love. I want to thank you for forgiving me for the hurt and pain that my disobedience has caused you. Thank you for being an example of how I should handle the offenses in my life. You are such a forgiving Father, and I am grateful that you love me and have forgiven me although I did not deserve it. In Jesus' name, amen!

Fruit of the Spirit – Gentleness

Where anger is a bursting flame, gentleness is a gentle rain.

- **Fr. John Hardon**

"I am sending you out like sheep among wolves. Therefore be as shrewd as snakes and as innocent as doves." **Matthew 10:16 (NIV)**

Being wise as serpents means to be wise, prudent and sensible. Additionally, it means that we are aware of what is in the best interest of all those involved.

Often, we are not mindful of just how gentleness can bring peace and calmness in the midst of chaos. Jesus was as gentle as a lamb, and He displayed His gentleness for all the world to see. He showed us gentleness when he washed the feet of His disciples. He shows his gentleness through His correction towards us when we disobey.

Although we may not be pleased with the consequences, He disciplines us in the most loving way. He is always there with open arms to console us, and He provides us with peace that surpasses all understanding, despite our wrongdoings. We should model ourselves after Jesus and display the same servant attitude towards our friends, family, husband and others. Our responses should display calmness. God himself spoke to Elijah as a gentle whisper (1 Kings 19:12). Therefore, we should mimic His gentleness as well.

When there are disagreements or conflicts that arise, we should recall Proverbs 15:1 (NIV) A gentle answer turns away wrath, but a harsh word stirs up anger.

God provided us with an escape that doesn't allow us to continue to provoke anger. Give a gentle approach and know when to remove yourself from the situation so that you remain obedient in how you should respond. Choose to become a representation of Jesus by upholding yourself in the highest regard so that your light shines through your response under unfavorable circumstances.

Through the gentleness of God's wisdom, we can learn how to express ourselves in a way that our responses aren't presented in offense, but in love. Gentleness has humility that carries a display of affection that is pleasing to the soul. Gentleness is rooted in acknowledging that the voice of God is speaking through you and acting on your behalf through the presence of the Holy Spirit.

Choose to walk in the Fruit of the Spirit that encompasses the wisdom that knows how to deal with conflict and frustration. Allow the gentle spirit of Jesus to be on full display so that you are a testament of how the Fruit of the Spirit can dwell inside of you and course correct with His love and His gentleness.

Prayer:

Dear God,

Thank you for displaying gentleness. Thank you for not being harsh or unkind to me, although I have often chosen to disobey your laws. Thank you for your course correction that was nothing short of pure love from a Father to His child. Thank you for gently loving me back into your arms and accepting me like the prodigal son. Thank you for reminding me that gentleness is not a sign of weakness but an indication of a level of unconditional love and self-control. In Jesus' name, amen!

Fruit of the Spirit – Faithfulness

Be faithful in small things, because it is in them that your strength lies.

- **Mother Teresa**

For the word of the Lord is right and true; He is faithful in all He does. **Psalm 33:4 (NIV)**

Our first commitment is to the Lord. We are to fear God and obey His commandments. And we are to follow His example.

Thus, we must first remain faithful to God. And we must remain faithful to our husbands.

Marriage should be honored by all, and the marriage bed kept pure, for God will judge the adulterer and all the sexually immoral.
Hebrews 13:4 (NIV)

As we prepare for marriage, we are tasked with understanding that faithfulness is a requirement within the covenant of marriage. In order to fully comprehend faithfulness, we must first become loyal to God. We have to sit in our trauma and trust that God is faithful to heal us and redeem us of our past transgressions.

Do this with the attitude that you are seeking a heart change. You are seeking more than just results - you are seeking a new life. We have to remain faithful to the process to improve in such a way that is pleasing to God and not to our flesh. Through our dedication to our Heavenly Father, we comprehend the covenant of faithfulness within marriage.

If your spouse should choose to be unfaithful, you still do not have permission to be unfaithful. Choose to remain obedient to our Father's commandments. Remember, you were first in covenant with God. Therefore, don't break your covenant with God as a way to get even.

The reality is that when we are mistreated, we fight to try to combat the mental anguish of the offense. We can find ourselves living in a mental torment of the circling thoughts that can paralyze us from making rational decisions.

Remember the Fruit of the Spirit and remember the Creator of the Fruit of the Spirit. Remember your covenant with Him and His faithfulness to you. Allow God to guide you through in a way that does not compromise your hard work and obedience

Choose to protect the mind, the body and the soul of your temple. Don't fight with your flesh, instead fight with your heart and choose to love yourself despite the choices that anyone else makes. Trust God in the season that you are facing and trust that you will reap a good harvest if you stand steadfast. Seek support from the Father to give you peace in the midst of any storm. Trust that He will calm the storm and provide you with the anchor that will keep you grounded. Stay faithful.

Prayer:

Dear God,

Thank you for your faithfulness. Thank you for being the one true Spirit that I can always rely on. Thank you for helping me to remain faithful. Thank you for sending your word to comfort me in the times when I was on the path to being unfaithful. Thank you for always remaining by my side and guiding me towards your loving arms when I was seeking to handle wrongdoing with ill intent. Thank you for never leaving my side. In Jesus' name, amen!

Fruit of the Spirit – Self-Control

Guard your tongue when your husband is angry.

- **St. Monica**

Like a city whose walls are broken through is a person who lacks self-control. Proverbs 25:28 (NIV)

A person who lacks self-control exposes their life to all kinds of temptations and danger.

My dear brothers and sisters, take note of this: Everyone should be quick to listen, slow to speak and slow to become angry, because human anger does not produce the righteousness that God desires.
James 1:19-20 (NIV)

What does it mean to have self-control? Self-control is defined as the ability to control oneself, in particular one's emotions and desires or the expression of them in one's behavior, especially in difficult situations.

There are three types of self-control: impulse control, emotional control, and movement control. Each of these plays a part in determining the outcome of a situation.

Impulsive behavior is the tendency to act without thinking. If you don't think before you speak or act, your impulsive thoughts can lead to overreacting. To combat impulsive behavior, take a second to shut down your thoughts when you feel threatened or provoked. Shift your focus to praying and asking God if you are about to overreact? Sit in silence and do not allow what is challenging this behavior to control you in this moment.

Failing to seek the mind of God when you are faced with major decisions is both foolish and sinful. Impulsive decisions can lead to sin. Be mindful that God requires us to be slow to speak and slow to anger. Acting off impulse leads to regret.

Additionally, be mindful of the tone that you are carrying as well. Once we spew out unkind words, they cannot be retracted. Allow your interaction with the Holy Spirit to align your thoughts and actions so that they are pleasing to God. In return, you won't regret your missteps, and you will also have pleased our Father in Heaven with your obedience.

Emotional control is often equally hard to manage. Too often, we experience an *emotional deluge*, also known as emotional flooding, a surge of intense emotions that can quickly overwhelm. In this overstimulated state, your body can shut down and it becomes difficult to manage your feelings or think clearly.

Many women have a hard time controlling this emotion. We were created with a flood of emotions and, if we're honest, our hormones don't play nice when our emotions become offended. It can become a challenge to not become overwhelmed emotionally when we are dealing with the matters of the heart. We desire empathy from our husband during this outpouring.

However, it can be challenging for men at times to connect with us emotionally. This is not an indication that they don't care how we are feeling at that moment. Instead, they simply are unsure of how to respond.

One way that we release our emotional deluge is through our tears. It can be difficult at times to express feelings that are buried deep within. Unfortunately, although Jesus understands our communication through our tears, our husband may not relate. He may empathize with the hurt, but we have to express ourselves with words and be as forthcoming as possible, in the kindest way. We can't become frustrated and overstimulate ourselves.

We can rely on God to provide the self-control we need.

2 Timothy 1:7 (NIV) For the Spirit God gave us does not make us timid, but gives us power, love and self-discipline.

Take a moment to step away from the conversation that is overwhelming you to regroup. Do not feel pressured to continue a conversation that you are not emotionally ready to have. Ask for time to pray and consult with God on how to continue when you are in a better headspace. Maybe you should choose to communicate through written communication versus continuing to verbally communicate if you are not making headway. Whatever you should choose, allow God to lead and not your emotions.

The third is movement control. This type of control is centered around body language. Often when we are expressing our point of view during a disagreement, we use harsh gestures and facial expressions. Pointing, obscene gesturing and uncontrolled facial expressions can lead to offense.

Be mindful of these offensive gestures, especially if this is something that you struggle with controlling. Acknowledge that this is an area that you are working on and accept accountability as the Holy Spirit continues to help you in this area. Allow in your heart a gentle correction from your husband so that you are reminded to reposition yourself. Don't allow his correction to offend you; instead accept it as accountability as you seek to self-correct these gestures on your own. Continue to pray and ask God to help you control this offense. Search for ways to improve in this area through scripture.

We are all a work in progress and some of the habits that we have allowed to control us, we are now being tasked to relinquish control of as we desire to release strongholds. The ultimate goal is to allow prayer to help us coagulate our weakness of self-control. Just as the blood of Jesus washes us white as snow, the Fruit of the Spirit provides control that produces better communication and a healthier marriage.

Prayer:

Dear God,

Help me control my emotions and any other areas in my life that I do not have control over. Please help me to be mindful of the things I say and the things that I do so that I can represent you in the most glorious light.

I will admit, I often lack self-control. Too often, I have chosen to control the outcome of conflict with my words and behavior verses controlling my tongue and my actions. Please help me stop "fueling the fire." Instead, provide me with control that, rather than reigniting the flame, allows the embers to burn out.

If there is anything that is preventing me from being the best part of me, I ask that you remove it now. I pray that you instill in me patience, gentleness and kindness as I work through this area of my life. I want to thank you for patiently waiting on me while I was in sin and displaying disobedience. Thank you for never leaving my side because I am lost without you. In Jesus' name, amen!

Fruit of the Spirit - Patience

The two most powerful warriors are patience and time.

- **Leo Tolstoy**

Not only so, but we also glory in our sufferings, because we know that suffering produces perseverance; perseverance, character; and character, hope. And hope does not put us to shame, because God's love has been poured out into our hearts through the Holy Spirit, who has been given to us. **Romans 5:3-5, (NIV)**

We have been taught that patience is a virtue.

What is a virtue? A virtue is the quality of being morally good.

What does it mean to be morally good? The definition of morally good is the state of possessing what is generally regarded as good character. Being rooted in virtue embraces a variety of characteristics, such as courage, justice, temperance and the like.

As many have experienced, our patience can be tested daily if we don't allow the Holy Spirit to dwell within us. Thus, the Fruit of the Spirit encompasses one another. If you have all of the Fruit of the Spirit, each of them carries a grace within each other. And that includes patience.

There are so many areas that require patience within our daily lives. For example, our patience is often tested when we are waiting for God to delicately place the husband we desire in our life.

Once we are united, we are tested with having patience as we attempt to navigate life together. We are tested to have patience with the differences of opinions. We are tested with learning how to handle one another's triggers and trauma. We are tested with patience as we wait to extend our family when it doesn't line up with our desired timeline. We are tested with patience when we want our spouse to mature in a manner that we think he should. We are tested during conflict to not say anything that could verbally hurt our husband and break down his self-esteem. We are tested in how to respect our husband as God instructed us within the Holy Bible.

We have a plethora of things that require our patience. But, once again, God reminds us that we can do what He asks.

Psalms 27:14 (NIV) Wait for the Lord; be strong, and take heart and wait for the Lord.

Our ultimate test of patience comes from our willingness to wait on God. We have to endure through the waiting. Do not become discouraged and eager for this to line up in the way that your flesh desires but patiently wait on God.

Philippians 4:6-7 (NIV) Do not be anxious about anything, but in every situation, by prayer and petition, with thanksgiving, present your requests to God. And the peace of God, which transcends all understanding, will guard your hearts and your minds in Christ Jesus.

Your patience will be required many days as you step into your role as wife and helpmeet. There will be days when you are partnering with your husband and the two of you do not see things for your household out of the same lens.

Therefore, I encourage you to remember to submit. Submit your thoughts to God and petition Him to come in and guide your heart and the heart of your husband. You both should submit to God and work together to resolve conflict.

Patience requires trust. You must trust in the Lord that, in due time, He will deliver the best results for you according to His perfect will for your life.

Marriage was designed to be a part of the Kingdom of God. Marriage is a relationship that is created to build oneness so that together we can shut down the plan and plots of the enemy.

Ecclesiastes 4:11-12 (NIV), Also, if two lie down together, they will keep warm. But how can one keep warm alone? Though one may be overpowered, two can defend themselves. A cord of three strands is not quickly broken.

Knowing that God has had so much patience with us throughout the duration of our lives, gives a different perspective to what is required of us when we are seeking to have patience with our spouse.

Marriage is bigger than self-gratification. It humbles you in the most unexpected ways. You gain an appreciation for the journey to love and the true meaning of servitude. You begin to find gratitude for the situations that try your patience the most.

It is of the utmost importance that you create a safe space within your marriage to patiently wait on one another to share and give perspective. In addition, you want to patiently allow one another to come to terms with things that are not done as you would expect or in the way that you would normally handle life. There is an adjustment period to understand one another's ebbs and flows.

Moreover, desire to understand with love and patience that your husband has his personal perspectives and his understanding of the directives that God has given to him on how to navigate life as the head of his family. Therefore, your patience is needed as he seeks God to become the husband that God created him to be.

Equally, be mindful that you also need your husband's patience as you continue to prepare to become his wife. As you seek to become a virtuous woman, rely on patience as you evolve mentally, spiritually and emotionally.

Prayer:

Holy God,

Thank you for your patience with me as I seek to become a virtuous woman. Thank you for your patience as I stumble and try to navigate through life. Thank you for your patience as I continue to make the same mistakes over and over again. Thank you for your patience as I seek to tame my tongue and become the Godly wife that you created me to be. Thank you for your patience as I seek to learn my role as a helpmeet. Guide me to how I can impact your Kingdom and teach my children, grandchildren and great-grandchildren to do the same. Thank you, God, for your overall patience with me. In Jesus' name, amen!

Preparing for Marriage

Marriage is more than having someone to be with until death do you part. It is far more than a fancy wedding gown, a ceremony filled with your closest friends and family, or a reception with food and celebratory music.

Marriage, in part, is an extension of God's covenant with Abraham. As part of that covenant, God expected that Abraham would be a faithful follower.

As we've learned, God's laws are based upon the obedience that He requires of His church. In addition to faithfulness, He desires us to be loving, caring, sharing, thriving, forgiving, patient, understanding, prayerful individuals with self-control. His expectation is that each person willingly works alongside one another, regardless of their individual differences.

As you prepare to become a wife, ask God to prepare your heart so that you remain steadfast through adversities and the overwhelming feeling of the demands and responsibilities that come along with the role of being a Godly helpmeet.

Remember that the same God who created you will be there to help you navigate your role as a wife.

"Before I formed you in the womb I knew you, before you were born, I set you apart; I appointed you as a prophet to the nations." **Jeremiah 1:5 (NIV)**

Therefore, we should go back to God, our manufacturer, and seek from Him the clarity on who He has called us to be. If God has called you to become a wife, seek His help in becoming the best wife you can possibly be. Deter from seeking knowledge that is not within the laws of what God so lovingly guides and tugs at your heart to do. Seek and listen to His instructions that are found within the Holy Bible. Seek to heal from past disappointments, trauma and unforgiveness that can bleed into your marriage. Heal your beautiful soul with the guidance of God Almighty, the Great I AM. Through healing, you will be ready and able to create a healthy marriage. Your desire should not only be to get married, but to stay married!

Preparing for Marriage – Trusting God While Remaining Patient

Do not be anxious about anything, but in every situation, by prayer and petition, with thanksgiving, present your requests to God. And the peace of God, which transcends all understanding, will guard your hearts and your minds in Christ Jesus. **Philippians 4:6-7 (NIV)**

Slow and steady… Preparation signifies your respect for the institution of marriage. Invite the Holy Spirit to guide you as you seek insight about your husband. This is the man that you are considering yoking with, procreating with and giving your heart to.

Because of the solemnity of this step, it is important that we trust that our Heavenly Father who created us is more than capable of uniting us with the right man. By seeking God's input, we can trust that he will find for each woman that man that fulfills us, that helps us flourish as we grow with him and with God. Seek the Creator and heed His obvious warnings. Don't be afraid to ask Him to open your eyes to see clearly. His input and guidance will help you see the things that have not been revealed that could separate you from His love, which is pivotal. As you seek to find love, don't neglect yourself and don't deny the intervention from Our Heavenly Father.

Make spending time daily with God nonnegotiable. Face your day by putting on the armor of God and it will become something that you thirst for and cannot live without. Ask God to help you readjust your mindset and bask in the beauty of your femininity. Work on healing so that you can trust again in the areas that you lost hope. Learn the power of forgiveness.

Your ultimate trust is in God and He remains faithful in healing us. Once you do the work within, you will continue to gain clarity on how to recognize the man that you should allow to pursue you.

In the meantime, continue to embrace your solitude. While Adam was in the Garden, he embraced solitude, not knowing that God planned to present Him with His helpmeet. In this season of preparation, you should not squander precious alone time. Prepare to balance this life and the busier days ahead once you are joined in Holy Matrimony. Stay committed to spending time daily with God to better understand how to navigate through life. The ultimate outcome should be to multiply and bring forth good fruit as a result of your union.

Prayer:

Dear Heavenly Father,

While in my season of being steadfast in my singleness, I vow to stay committed to you. I vow to be obedient and exhibit behavior that is pleasing to you. I understand that my first covenant is with you. You are the ultimate Bridegroom, my best friend and my provider. Help me to understand my purpose and allow me to remain focused on your perfect plan for me. While I am waiting, help me to work on healing the dark places that have me bound. Allow me to forgive and love like you Lord. I am grateful for this time of singleness as I am allowed more intimate time with you. Help me to understand your timing is perfect and that you are the strength of my life. As long as I have you, I have everything that I need. In Jesus' name, amen!

Preparing for Marriage – Premarital Counseling

> He who finds a wife finds what is good and receives favor from the LORD. **Proverbs 18:22 (NIV)**

Seeking premarital counseling prior to marriage is a personal choice.

There should be careful consideration placed into choosing the counselor that will support your personal healing and preparation for your covenant with your husband.

First and foremost, seek guidance from the Holy Spirit for His direction. Many accredited therapists have the knowledge and experience to introduce you to the general aesthetics of marriage and family counseling based upon what studies have deemed as "the standard." But the one true counselor is our Heavenly Father.

Choosing to work with a spiritual counselor who prioritizes God as their Lord and Savior and uses the Bible for reference can help shine light on God's principles. In addition, that counselor's advice will be Bible based and lead you back to the source--our Heavenly Father--to continue to seek inner healing.

Within the Holy Bible, there are precise instructions on how we are to operate as husband and wife through the help of the Fruit of the Spirit. With these spiritual qualities, and through the help of the Holy Spirit, we can work in unity to provide a loving and peaceful environment for our family. There are Biblical examples of God's plan for families.

Your wife will be like a fruitful vine within your house; your children will be like olive shoots around your table. Yes, this will be the blessing for the man who fears the Lord. **Psalm 128: 3-4 (NIV)**

Needless to say, before your husband finds you, you should seek to find yourself. Team up with the Holy Spirit through repentance and seek to become a better version of yourself by seeking to heal from any past trauma that caused you heartache and frustration. Trust in the healing process and seek to become the version of yourself that not only your husband can be grateful for, but that you can be proud of!

Personal Testimony:

I have sought counseling for years. I have sought individual counseling as well as couples counseling. I personally have found individual counseling more helpful and here's why: I needed to work on myself! I had not healed enough to take on couples counseling and, as a result, it turned into "the blame game." I often left couples counseling feeling more upset than I did before the session. Therefore, I suggest working on yourself first and foremost.

Seek a spiritual counselor who can provide you scripture for self-reflection and self-healing. Dig into the root cause of your personal trauma and obstacles so you gain a clearer mindset of who you are. Then, if you should pursue couples counseling, you can speak of your shortcomings, as well as your boundaries.

The work does not begin when you are married. The work begins prior to marriage. Consistently dedicate time for self-improvement. If you aren't dedicated to working to improve, you are proving that you aren't dedicated. Let's work…on ourselves!

Preparing for Marriage – Be You

It is important that you are always your authentic self. Do not pretend to be anyone that you are not.

I praise you because I am fearfully and wonderfully made; your works are wonderful, I know that full well. **Psalm 139:14 (NIV)**

Be honest about the things that you can and cannot do well so that you do not set up false expectations of who you truly are to your husband. Begin your relationship just how you choose to live within your relationship. Avoid pretense. For example, you might be tempted to pretend to be a woman who enjoys cooking seven days a week, even when cooking is not your forte. This is fake; you are pretending to be what you think he wants or needs. If you lure him in with unintentional service, you are creating a false sense of servitude. You are starting the marriage off as a lie.

Remember that you were uniquely and wonderfully made. Therefore, if you are not interested in a household chore, communicate this before you enter into the covenant of marriage.

As a helpmeet, we are called to help meet daily needs of the household. While being a wife does not come with the mandate of cooking and cleaning, God did call the man to labor. Your husband will be working to fulfill the vision that God has given him. Therefore, as the wife, you will need to step in as the teammate to help keep things in order inside the home. Discuss what that will look like for your marriage. But don't pretend that you are capable of fulfilling roles that you are not.

If you are also employed outside the home, discuss the possibility of the two of you working together to complete daily tasks. This will help create open communication and peace within your home. The conversation can also help minimize burnout. Discuss divvying up the work so that neither of you become overwhelmed with a never-ending daunting list of chores.

Many were taught as young children that sharing is caring. Implement this principle within your marriage, especially as it relates to household work. Sharing is caring extends beyond the thought of money and materialistic things. Allow this coined phrase to apply to ideas, chores, feelings and our love for our Heavenly Father.

Couples share most everything in the marriage. In each union, spouses share the same space within the home. They also share child(ren), the same bed, food, bills, desires, ups and downs, and many hopes and dreams; the list goes on and on. We share so much of ourselves, both physically and emotionally. How can we share our strengths and weaknesses? How can we share our best practices with one another so that we benefit from the knowledge and wisdom of what has been imparted in us that has helped us be successful thus far? Seek God and He will guide you!

Personal Testimony:

I had to be ok with being me. I no longer wanted to pretend to like foods, places or things just because that was something that my love interest liked. If I wasn't interested in something, I no longer wanted to pretend just to be more likable. I wanted to authentically be me! I didn't have an interest in cooking and, early on, when my husband and I were dating, I expressed this. My disinterest in cooking did not make me feel less than the woman that God created me to be.

On the contrary, my husband has a passion for cooking and is also a chef! I just knew my prayers had been answered when he shared this with me :)

Needless to say, I shared what I desired to do within the home. I wanted to be forthcoming in hopes of avoiding doing unwanted domestic chores with a begrudging attitude. In terms of cooking, we balanced this task with him agreeing to cook most of the meals while I, in turn, would work beside him and keep the kitchen clean.

We also understand that this plan won't work 365 days a year. Life throws curve balls, and we need to shift expectations when those commitments are impossible.

As we started discussions, I was not going to pretend to be a wife that wanted to be in the kitchen daily preparing meals just to appease him. Although I do not cook most of the meals, I will prepare and cook meals when needed because of busy schedules. Or I can opt to order take out! This became an acknowledged standard operation within our home, and I am so grateful I chose to authentically be me.

Preparing for Marriage - Communication

The wise in heart accept commands, but a chattering fool comes to ruin. **Proverbs 10:8 (NIV)**

If we are committed to being vulnerable about who we authentically are, we should think about how we can share by communicating more intimately.

In choosing this path, we become a representative of our Father in Heaven. Proverbs 15:1-2 (NIV) A gentle answer turns away wrath, but a harsh word stirs up anger. The tongue of the wise adorns knowledge, but the mouth of the fool gushes folly. Communication is key in marriage and is needed to function daily throughout life. Working on our communication skills will help us better express ourselves and help us filter out frustration, anxiety and any issues that lay dormant within. Through seeking the guidance of the Holy Spirit daily, He helps us to reflect love within our marriage.

Take the time to rest with our Father in Heaven before bringing up hard topics. Allow the Holy Spirit to guide the conversation so that your words and emotions become like the balm of Gilead.

Taking time to ponder a response, and seeking God's input before replying, helps us become better skilled at expressing how we are feeling. Choose to express yourself with kindness and gentleness. Don't allow resentment to fester and cause an outburst of displaced emotions. Don't assume the worst about a situation, first take time to communicate with your husband about the situation. Effectively communicating with love allows us to listen to one another, which will in turn help us segue towards a resolution.

Communication is especially critical in allowing you to be you.

The role of a woman is often underestimated because many women tend to make it look so easy. In reality, most couples would say living together is not instantly easy. There are conversations that need to be had prior to combining households. We often fall in love with the idea of love. It's only later that we realize love is not enough to combat the massive emotions we feel performing "wifely" duties day after day.

Take the time while single to be honest about the chores you can perform on a day-to-day basis. Have an open and honest conversation with your husband or potential husband surrounding expectations of the daily chores that both of you are capable of fulfilling.

As part of preparation, it is important to hold these conversations prior to the "I do." The goal is to eliminate the frustration that can be internalized and then presented later in anger. When discussing anything important, be honest about your expectations. You should expect the same open communication from your husband. Talk about what the standard operating procedures will be for your home and how you can equally conquer house chores and financial responsibilities. Create a plan with the understanding that unforeseen circumstances can arrive and you are both open to additional dialogue if and when needed.

The key is keeping yourself available to open communication. Communicate your expectations and long-term goals for your marriage. Do not allow the fear of an argument to hold you back from expressing your aspirations. Remember the Fruit of the Spirit, then allow gentleness and kindness to help guide you into a colloquy that creates peace, love and honesty.

Personal Testimony:

I was fortunate to have been raised with a mother who not only held a 9-5 job but also managed to nurture my dad within our home. My mom cooked, cleaned, and poured her love, knowledge and wisdom into our family. She set for me a strong foundation of what being a wife entails. As I shared earlier, there are some things that I do not desire to take on because I am authentically me. But I am ever so grateful that she was a great example of how to cleave to your husband. She positioned herself in such a way that I now comprehend that those traits were examples of a Proverbs 31 woman. She was loving, gentle, kind, patient and self-controlled in many areas of her life.

As a result of her example, I also became a nurturer to my husband. As part of that care, I desire to take care of his emotional health. I desired to pour into him to help him endure the daily grind of what I know very little about… being a man in this cold world. It's the love of a woman that filters and refines. It's choosing to create peace and structure inside your home that will sustain your husband and allow him to labor for the household. His labor of love is outside of the home and as a wife; my labor of love is within the home.

I am learning to **leave** behind the things that I saw growing up that will not serve God in my home. I am choosing to **cleave** to the knowledge and wisdom that God is teaching me to create peace within my home. It's not an easy task and I work on this daily. However, all things are possible with the help of the Holy Spirit.

Preparing for Marriage – Friendships

Although we tend to share quite a few things within the marriage, there are also things that we don't share. Friendship interests might fit in that category. We may have developed a lasting friendship with someone that our spouse does not like. How do you handle those relationships?

This issue can arise whether the person is of the same or opposite sex. But the issue can be even more contentious when the person is of the opposite sex. Do you end relationships of the opposite sex that make your spouse uncomfortable? Each person's perspective varies on how these friendships should be handled.

Often there is guilt that can lead to coercion that somehow manipulates the other spouse into agreeing to friendships that they are uncertain about. Additionally, there could be a scathing boundary that reinforces a rebellious spirit to give in to what may seem like "control" from their spouse.

As you navigate the issue, it is important to consider the perspective of your spouse so that early on you gain their trust and diminish unnecessary conflict within the marriage. Open communication and understanding are required.

When you covenant with your husband, you vow to forsake all others. You should carefully consider how to navigate outside relationships that could cause strife within your marriage. Consider the importance of the union that you vowed to and work towards making your husband your best friend.

This is not to say that you should not have friends. However, evaluate your circle and make wise decisions regarding whom you can trust in all aspects as it pertains to your union. Allow the Spirit to guide you during these tough reflections and the conversations that follow. Use the Fruit of the Spirit to express how uncomfortable any current friendship relationships make you feel.

If you have not had the opportunity to meet his friends, take the time to openly discuss the types of friendships that you currently value and discuss the impact they may have in your marriage. Good friends are hard to find but Godly friends are even harder. Choose your friendships wisely and choose to kindly express what's on your heart without jealousy or malice intent.

Proverbs 16:24 (NIV) Gracious words are a honeycomb, sweet to the soul and healing to the bones.

Ask God to help you become the best friend that your husband needs and desires. Work to harmonize and foster outside friendships that will help cultivate your union. In return, allow your union to do the same for the friendships that you both agree are suitable for how each of you are choosing to serve within God's Kingdom.

Personal Testimony:

In my personal experience, having friends of the opposite sex can cause issues in a marriage. I understand that we can't avoid dealing with the opposite sex in our daily lives. However, there are boundaries that we should discuss with our husband to ensure that we don't cross unchartered territory. I understand scenarios, such as, he was your friend before you were married. However, what if that male friend makes your husband uncomfortable?

Your vow was to forsake all others. What does that mean in this instance?

I personally feel as though you have to be forthcoming about the relationship and if you have been romantic or thought about being romantic with your friend. You should also discuss whether your friend has, or ever had, romantic feelings for you. If yes, don't be disrespectful and introduce him to your husband as just a friend. Keep your side of the marriage clean! Don't allow the enemy to sneak in through any cracks.

I understand that it is hard to lose friends that you have grown to love and care for over the years. However, if any of your friends, male or female, should cause discomfort in your marriage, you should look to resolve the disagreement with your husband first and foremost. Both you and your friend should have the emotional intelligence to understand that you are embarking on a new journey in your life and your time and season has ended.

You have chosen to take on a sacred covenant under God. Therefore, what once may have served you in life before the "I do," now requires levels of reconsideration.

I personally chose to cut off friendships with the opposite sex. That decision was a lesson learned from past relationships. There were always issues caused by opposite-sex friendships. This was especially true with male friends that failed to toe the line. If your love interest expresses any discomfort with your friends, you owe him a level of understanding.

In my second marriage, I just refused to further engage in such relationships if there had been any previous involvement or chance that any disrespect could occur. I did not want to establish a foundation that could invite an opportunity for temptation.

By no means am I advocating for you to abandon your friend(s). On the contrary, it means that you are emotionally intelligent enough to have the awareness and maturity to choose to prioritize your husband. In addition, you defeat any plots that the enemy could try to use through those friendships to gain a foothold into your ordained marriage.

Preparing for Marriage – Being a Helpmeet

As a helpmeet, our role is to serve our husband. We help him in areas that we see a need with our physical hands and also with our responses, attitudes and, most critically, our prayers. We are to become willing vessels throughout the journey of marriage. Become willing to exhibit a loving response and attitude as we allow God to mold us into the wife that He created us to be.

As a wife, we are emulating the characteristics of the Holy Spirit. We are called to resemble the love of our Heavenly Father. The Fruit of the Spirit helps to outline that directive.

It is love that fuels the hearts of our husband. When we are loving him in the way that God created us to, our love transforms and motivates. The Holy Spirit stands in the midst of our marriage and strengthens us. God helps us to endure struggles by providing us with patience. Through our obedience and willingness to bear these fruits, we are covered under the protection of our Heavenly Father.

Seek to work at building your relationship with God. Invite the Holy Spirit to dwell inside of you. Use the gifts of the Holy Spirit to advocate on your behalf to help bind any spirit that is within you or your husband that is not pleasing to God. Pray daily without ceasing for a fruitful marriage.

But the Advocate, the Holy Spirit, whom the Father will send in my name, will teach you all things and will remind you of everything I have said to you. **John 14:26 (NIV)**

We can gently ask the Holy Spirit to act on our behalf as the advocate during marital situations where we are uncomfortable or are having difficulty reaching our husband's heart. As an obedient, renewed vessel, the Holy Spirit dwells inside of you. You have an advocate and a counselor that is with you daily to help assist you.

In the same way, the Spirit helps us in our weakness. We do not know what we ought to pray for, but the Spirit himself intercedes for us through wordless groans. **Romans 8:26 (NIV)**

These scriptures are a reminder to tap into what God has already made available to you--His spirit that dwells inside of you. With the help of the Holy Spirit, you are able to do exceedingly and abundantly above all that you can ask or think.

Now to him who is able to do immeasurably more than all we ask or imagine, according to his power that is at work within us. **Ephesians 3:20 (NIV).**

Personal Testimony:

I was unaware of what it meant to be a helpmeet. I was unaware of what my role as a wife entailed. I was oblivious to what was truly needed of me on a day-to-day basis…until I sought God!

As a helpmeet, I am here to serve. God created me in a way to serve not just with my body, but with my heart and mind. I am here to "meet" my husband's shortcomings. I am here to "meet" him when he is struggling spiritually, physically, financially and mentally. I am here to "meet" his needs in a way that causes him to reciprocate and meet my needs as well.

I had to lay down my selfishness and pick up the Fruit of the Spirit. I had to trust that if I am doing what God has asked me to do and, if in return, I do not receive what I need from my husband, My Heavenly Father will still meet my needs. Therefore, I am never at a loss. My past actions were to shut down and refuse to do anything when I was upset with my husband. However, I realized that this was not pleasing to God. I can only be responsible for my actions. I had a choice to make; if I wanted to see different results, I had to do something different.

My past actions had not yielded good fruit. In fact, the fruit was outright rotten at times. I wanted to reap a good harvest, so I was tasked to plant good seeds. I began working to plant seeds of love, joy, peace, kindness, gentleness, forgiveness, patience, faithfulness and self-control. In return, my husband also began to plant those same seeds. Although we remained a work in progress, thankfully, I was able to witness water on barren land and fruit of new beginnings.

Preparing for Marriage – Choices

God gives us free will. We can choose all sorts of things in life. We choose what we want to eat, where we want to live, who we want to be friends with, and the list goes on and on.

One thing that we should not seek to choose is the man whom we should marry. We obviously have the choice to choose him in reciprocation. However, we should not choose to pursue a man. The man should choose to pursue you, and you should choose whether or not you want to be pursued. Do not go out of God's order and choose to take on the role of a man. If you should choose to do so, you are choosing to assist God instead of trusting God to assist you.

He who finds a wife finds what is good and receives favor from the Lord. **Proverbs 18:22 (NIV)**

Note that the Scripture says it is he who finds a wife, and not she that finds a husband.

Choose for yourselves this day whom you will serve. **Joshua 24:15 (NIV)**

Choose to stay in order. Choose to follow the guidance and the path of direction that God has provided. The choice is yours!

Personal Testimony:

I have had my sights set on someone whom I thought I should pursue in hopes that the end result would render me a wife in his eyes. However, I found that I was going ahead of God and doing the pursuing instead of being the one who is pursued. I should have been patient and trusted that, in time, God would send me His best. As a result, I would have clearly seen that the one who I was attempting to pursue was honestly just not that interested in pursuing me.

I discovered the truth of Myles Munroe's quote, "If you leave the presence of God to go and find a male, you have discovered a malfunctioning male."

I now understand that I should not force myself upon a man in hopes that he will see me as a wife. Women should allow the man to organically pursue and be intentional in doing so. When there is a mutual attraction, it is liberating when a man is pursuing you as his love interest. It is also one of the giddiest feelings to be asked on a date, given flowers and then asked, "when can I see you again"?

You don't have to chase who's chasing you. You don't have to worry if he is interested because, if he is, you won't second-guess his intentions. You don't have to worry if he is the one. You won't have to make excuses because he will show up and show you that you are the one that he chooses. Choose to be pursued.

Preparing for Marriage – Order

From the beginning of time, God established order here on Earth. He created the world in chronological order. He created what and who was put on Earth and he determined the order in which he created it. Likewise, He created the man before He created the woman. God created the man to labor and tend to the animals and the land. In addition, God created man as the head of the home.

Next, the woman was created and placed inside of the kingdom to help create order within the home. She was given birthing rights and dominion over her children alongside her husband. She was to assist with the establishment of order within the home while the husband was out laboring to provide for the things that would go inside of the home.

This order created a dynamic duo. It is the order in which we should build our foundation. Choose to marry a man whom you can submit to as the head of household. Choose to marry a man that is aware of his role and who seeks God so that you can also fulfill your role within the home. Both individuals within the marriage have equally important roles to play so that they can flourish within God's kingdom. These roles establish the order of operations within the home. You are both equally a boss in your own right; however, there is only one true head of household!

The order that God established and set for households will help create a foundation to build upon. In His order, no one is greater than the other. The two of you are in a partnership and the focus is to work together. However, the establishment of order creates an understanding of the responsibilities within the home. This is to help ensure that the household operates at its intended capacity.

Personal Testimony:

After my first marriage failed, and I became the only one managing my home, I considered myself, "the head of the household." I became what many refer to as a strong independent woman. I was so used to doing things "my" way that, during my second marriage, I was unable to take off my head-of-household hat and allow my husband full reign.

This resulted in my husband often feeling disrespected. Initially, I was unsure what I was doing wrong, as I was only trying to help! I had become so accustomed to doing things "my way" that I didn't understand how "my way" was now considered out of order!

As a result, my husband and I butted heads. It wasn't until I read the Holy Bible that I began to comprehend the correct order. God decreed that each home must have order in order to function at its fullest capacity. And he established what that order should be. It required me to learn that order yields respect. God's order helps establish for each of us the roles He has given within the home.

We have a choice to choose "our way" or "God's way". Understanding that the Creator of the universe is well aware of what is needed within His Kingdom, I decided to abide by His laws. This does not mean that I don't have the ability to rule and reign in my home. It just means that I respect both the Creator and my husband. Therefore, as a result of me yielding to God's order, His way helps minimize disorder and disagreements. As a result, there is more peace, love and joy. I will gladly trade my boss hat any day to indulge in those delectable fruits!

Your marriage is the guidepost by which your children will establish their standards for their own marriage.

- Catherine Hickem

Workbook - Self-Reflection Questions to Answer Before Marriage

1. Why are you seeking to become a wife?

2. What responsibilities will you take on as a helpmeet?

3. How effective are you at communicating and how can you improve?

4. What are some past hurts that you are holding on to that you should consider seeking healing from (i.e., traumatic experience, unforgiveness, unresolved issues from heartache and trust issues). Now that you have recognized them, what

can you do to begin healing internally?

5. What are your social media boundaries and how can you work on exercising a healthy use of social media?

6. What is your plan of action when you are in an emotional crisis with your husband during times of disagreements?

7. What are some ways you desire to resolve conflict? How can you seek God during those times that you are unable to resolve conflict on your own?

8. How are you choosing to spend time with God daily?

9. How can you increase spending time with God daily?

10. How are you seeking to understand what it means to be in covenant with God?

11. What does it mean to forsake all others?

12. What are some things that you would like to implement into your home as standard operating procedures once you are in a covenant marriage?

13. What are some boundaries that you can set in place to ensure that you and your husband have uninterrupted time

alone? i.e., no outside phone conversations or television or phone after a certain hour.

14. If you are currently a wife, how can you prepare to become a better wife?

15. After you become a wife, how can you evaluate yourself to improve as a helpmeet in the upcoming years?

16. What do you have in place or what can you put in place, as a failsafe to reduce conflict within your marriage?

17. What are some things that you can do or work on to show respect for your husband?

18. As a helpmeet, what are some spiritual, physical and emotional areas that you can work on to help eliminate burnout in your husband? (i.e., prayer, helping with additional household chores, understanding when to bring up tough conversations when he has expressed that he is emotionally exhausted)

19. What are some things that you need in order to feel loved?

20. How do you recognize when you are not feeling loved? How will you express that feeling with your husband?

Workbook - Discussion Questions for a Couple

Use this section to create a list of premarital questions. Think of things that are important to you and how you would like to implement those things in your marriage. Pray and seek God on how you will come to an agreement so that there is clarity on how the other views these issues. Openly welcome topics of concern from your future husband as well. I have compiled a list of a few topics to help you get started:

Communication:

- How would you define effective communication?
- When you were growing up, how did your parents(s) or guardian(s) communicate with each other and with you?
- What makes you shut down during communication?
- How can I best communicate with you?
- When should I not communicate with you?

Girls Night/Boys Night Out

- How do you feel about girls night/boys night out?
- What is considered a respectable time to be home?
- How often should you hang out with your friends without your spouse?
- How do you make your spouse feel comfortable while you are away on outings with friends?

Vacationing with Friends of the Same Sex

- Discuss what makes each of you uncomfortable as it relates to a girls trip or guys trip, involving at least one night away.
- Is vacationing with friends of the same sex allowed?
- If yes, is there a limit on how often and for how long?
- Does a yes include traveling out of the country with friends of the same sex?

Friendships with the Opposite Sex

- Discuss what makes each of you uncomfortable as it relates to opposite sex friendships openly and honestly.
- Is it okay to have friendships with people of the opposite sex after marriage?
- Is it okay to have text exchanges with friends of the opposite sex? If yes, how are those conversations shared with your spouse?
- Is it okay to go to lunch or dinner with friends of the opposite sex without your spouse?

Vacations for Just the Couple

- Discuss your expectations of vacations with your spouse. Consider budget concerns, as well as the types of vacations you wish to experience - from the beach to the mountains, from deserts to foreign countries.
- How often do you expect to vacation with one another?
- How long is each trip?
- Where do you want to vacation?
- Who chooses where you as a couple will vacation?
- Discuss what type of vacation you wish to experience - whether action-packed with lots of physical adventures, a culturally enriching experience visiting museums and learning history, or a get-away-from-it-all rest and relaxation time away from everyone.

Family of Origin (the family where you were raised)

- What does your family of origin mean to each of you respectively?
- Talk about growing up as a child and who helped shape who you are today.
- What effective communication styles did you witness growing up? If communication was not effective, what would have helped?
- How would you like to spend time with your family of origin (phone conversations, holidays, regular meals/visits, etc.)
- What are your expectations for incorporating your family of origin into the family that you are building with your spouse?
- What role do you expect your spouse to have with your family of origin?

Finances

- How are you each financially? What are your credit scores?
- If either person has a low credit score/financial problems, what are the plans to correct those scores?
- Discuss how bills will be paid when you are married.
- Discuss whether you will keep separate or joint banking accounts.
- Discuss how you will handle previous assets or debts that are brought into the marriage.
- Discuss savings accounts and how they will be used.
- Discuss outstanding debt and the plan to clear it up.
- Discuss with honesty your weakness when it comes to finances.
- Discuss how you will handle financial challenges, such as job loss.

Children

- Discuss how many children each of you would like to have.
- If you want children together, when do you want them? Immediately? Or after a specific timeframe or milestone?
- If either of you have children from a previous relationship, discuss how you envision co-parenting.
- If you both want children, but have not conceived within the timeframe discussion, what other options would you like to consider, if any?
- Who is responsible for the children in terms of discipline?
- Who is responsible for a child in terms of basic care, such as feeding, baths, and bedtime?
- When the child is older, who is responsible for homework and extracurricular activities?
- Discuss your thoughts on a stay-at-home parent vs. a nanny or in-home daycare vs. a public daycare.
- Discuss your opinions on private, public or homeschool education for your child.

Health

- Discuss your thoughts centered around regular healthcare visits.
- Discuss the importance of eating healthily and annual checkups.
- Discuss who will schedule appointments for annual checkups and dental exams.
- How do we deal with short term and long-term illnesses.
- Discuss who will carry/pay for the medical and dental insurance.

Church/Serving God

- Discuss what church you will attend once you are married.

- How often will you go to church?
- Discuss options for serving God within your home. Will you pray before every meal? At bedtime? Will you pray together or alone? Couple or family Bible Study?
- How will you signal that you are purposely studying or worshiping alone with God?

Pets

- If one of you currently has a pet, discuss how that pet will be handled once you are married. Will the person who currently owns the pet maintain responsibility for its care? Does that include the pets' expenses (i.e., food, pet insurance, toys, bed, grooming, boarding)?
- If you don't have a pet, what are your thoughts on having one? What kind? And when?
- How will you divide up the responsibilities of caring for the pet?

Holidays/Birthdays

- What holidays do you like to celebrate and how do you like to celebrate them?
- What are the holidays that you do not like to celebrate?
- Discuss what holidays, if any, are extended to a larger definition of family, such as parents or siblings.
- How do you like to celebrate your birthday?

Togetherness

- Discuss your perspective on date nights.
- Discuss how you prioritize maintaining a healthy work-life balance
- How often is date night in terms of weeks or months?
- Who is responsible for scheduling date nights? And does scheduling include generating ideas?

- What are the types of date nights - outside of the home or in the home - that you prefer?
- Consider making a list of date night ideas to keep for future use.
- How will you commit to spending intimate time with one another?
- How will you set aside distractions and overcome fatigue or other responsibilities?

Rest/Downtime

- What is your definition of rest or downtime?
- How important is rest to you?
- How often do you desire to work before seeking a vacation or a day off?
- What are your thoughts about the commandment to "Remember the Sabbath Day and keep it Holy"?

Disagreements

- If we are unable to resolve conflict, how do we come to terms so that we do not allow the conflict to affect us? Do we agree to revisit the conflict within 24-48 hours? Do we default to writing our feelings out vs verbal communication so that we are both heard?
- What are your thoughts on premarital and marriage counseling? How often do you feel that counseling is needed? (i.e., once a year, for 3 months, only when there is conflict, I don't believe in counseling; we can seek to resolve our own issues,)

Household Chores

- Who do you think should be responsible for cooking meals?
- Who do you think should be responsible for cleaning the house? Are there certain tasks that should be split - for

example, one person cooks and the other cleans the kitchen?
- Who do you think should be responsible for buying groceries? Who should put the groceries away in its proper place?
- Do you believe that household chores can be divided between both the husband and wife? Do you believe that the husband and wife can work together to complete house chores? Should the children be involved in helping with household chores?
- What cohesive plan can be implemented for household chores to decrease burnout?

Intimacy

- What is your definition of intimacy?
- How often do you desire sexual intercourse? How often do you desire intimacy that does not involve sexual intercourse?
- Do you prefer that your spouse initiates sexual intercourse, or would you rather be the one to initiate?
- What makes you uncomfortable in the bedroom?
- What makes you comfortable in the bedroom?
- Was there any trauma that you may have experienced as a child or young adult that you need to discuss that is relative to the way you view sex and intimacy?

*** **Please be willing to exercise the Fruit of the Spirit when discussing trauma. This is a very sensitive topic.*****

Epilogue

In closing, while in your season of preparation, it is imperative that you reflect on the standard operating procedures that you desire for your home. Moreover, prepare your mind by seeking God to heal your heart from past traumas. Often, we establish our home based upon what is socially acceptable or what we witnessed in our upbringing as children. Those standard operating procedures that may have worked for your parents, grandparent or guardian(s) may not work for you; if they do not, they should not become a staple in your home. Therefore, decide what will work effectively to create peace, love and joy within your Garden of Eden.

- What are your heart's desires when you vision the operation within your home?
- Is your vision realistic?
- Are you willing to compromise with your husband and willing to exercise patience and forgiveness as you work through these desires?

Clarifying your roles within the home prior to marriage will circumvent chaos. It is imperative that you remember to exercise self-control as you navigate through personal perspectives of what roles a husband and wife should fill within the home. Remember kindness, faithfulness and gentleness are also characteristics of our Father in Heaven. If you desire to become a Proverbs 31 woman, study her ideal characteristics and pray for God to create in you the Godly attributes through the Fruit of the Spirit.

Prayer:

Our Heavenly Father,

Thank you for preparing me to become a wife. I recognize that there were things that I was not knowledgeable of and areas where I was lacking that could prevent me from being the helpmeet that you created me to be. Continue to open my eyes to this beautiful idea of marriage and help me to become a better version of myself day by day.

As I strive to be more like the idea of the Proverbs 31 woman, please increase my territory so that I can share my knowledge and wisdom with other young ladies who also have the same desire. I pray that I can represent your namesake well. In Jesus' name, amen!

About the Author

Felicia Ann is a redeemed woman of God, a devoted mother, and a spiritual encourager whose greatest joy is walking alongside women as they prepare their hearts for God-centered love and marriage. Born from personal heartache and spiritual revelation, her debut book Preparing to Become a Bride by Studying the Fruit of the Spirit is a testimony of transformation—from brokenness to purpose, from confusion to clarity, through the power of Yah's love.

Raised by hardworking, visionary parents—a trailblazing Black entrepreneur and a devoted educator-she learned the value of faith, perseverance, and purpose. But it wasn't until she surrendered to Christ that she truly began to understand her identity as a daughter of the King and the sacred calling of becoming not just being—a wife.

Deeply inspired by her children and guided by God's Word, she now uses her writing and ministry to uplift women in all stages of life, reminding them that healing is possible, joy is real, and agape love is within reach. She honors those who walked with her through the darkness, and now humbly walks in the light of Yah's faithfulness.

For inquiries related to bookings and life coaching sessions, or to purchase books and merchandise, please visit:

HisHelpmeet.org

www.ingramcontent.com/pod-product-compliance
Lightning Source LLC
Chambersburg PA
CBHW070853050426
42453CB00012B/2167